CHARLES De PAOLO

Coleridge: Historian of Ideas

English Literary Studies
University of Victoria
1992

ENGLISH LITERARY STUDIES
Published at the University of Victoria

FOUNDER AND GENERAL EDITOR
Samuel L. Macey

EDITORIAL BOARD
Patricia J. Köster
Victor A. Neufeldt
Terry G. Sherwood
Reginald C. Terry

ADVISORY EDITORS
David Fowler, *University of Washington*
Donald Greene, *University of Southern California*
Juliet McMaster, *University of Alberta*
Richard J. Schoeck, *University of Colorado*
Arthur Sherbo, *Michigan State University*

BUSINESS MANAGER
Hedy Miller

ISBN 0-920604-60-9

The ELS Monograph Series is published in consultation with members of the Department by ENGLISH LITERARY STUDIES, Department of English, University of Victoria, B.C., Canada, V8W 3P4.

ELS Monograph Series No. 54
© 1992 by Charles De Paolo

To Erica

CONTENTS

	Acknowledgements	7
	Abbreviations	8
	Preface	10
CHAPTER ONE	Introduction	11
TWO	The Development of Universal History	14
THREE	Chiliastic Verse	24
FOUR	Reaction Against the Enlightenment: The "Canonization" of Edward Gibbon	29
FIVE	"A Wonderful Accordance": The Figural Method	37
SIX	"The Great Drama of the World": The Idea of Providence	43
SEVEN	"Of Union and Ennoblement": Ancient and Classical History	49
EIGHT	"The Lessons of Wisdom and Caution": European History, Medieval to Modern	65
NINE	The Ideas of Church and State	87
TEN	The Problem of Historical Knowledge	99
	Notes	103

ACKNOWLEDGEMENTS

Over its eight-year gestation, this study has benefited from sound advice and owes more to others than can be accurately recounted. For direction and encouragement, I thank those who read early and late drafts of the manuscript or who commented on articles drawn from it: Robert O. Preyer, Henry Kozicki, Stuart Peterfreund, Marilyn Gaull, Paul Magnuson, Laurence Lockridge, Anya Taylor, J. Robert Barth, S.J., Arthur Young, Robert Zweig, and Samuel Macey. Parts of this book have appeared in journals, and I also thank the editors for granting permission to reprint: Marilyn Gaull, *The Wordsworth Circle*, copyright © Marilyn Gaull; Stuart Peterfreund, *Nineteenth-Century Contexts*, copyright © Interdisciplinary Nineteenth-Century Studies; and Henry Kozicki, *CLIO*, copyright © Robert H. Canary and Henry Kozicki. Oxford University Press granted permission to quote from *The Collected Letters of Samuel Taylor Coleridge*, edited by Earl Leslie Griggs, copyright © 1956-1971 by Oxford University Press; and from *Coleridge: Poetical Works*, edited by Ernest Hartley Coleridge, copyright © 1912 (reprinted 1967) by Oxford University Press. And I thank Princeton University Press for permission to quote from *The Collected Notebooks of Samuel Taylor Coleridge*, copyright © 1957- by Princeton University Press, as well as from the following volumes of *The Collected Works of Samuel Taylor Coleridge: The Friend*, ed. Barbara E. Rooke, copyright © 1969 by Princeton University Press; *Lectures 1795: On Politics and Religion*, eds. Lewis Patton and Peter Mann, copyright © 1971 by Princeton University Press; *Lay Sermons*, ed. R. J. White, copyright © 1972 by Princeton University Press; *On the Constitution of the Church and State*, ed. John Colmer, copyright © 1976 by Princeton University Press; the *Marginalia*, ed. George Whalley, copyright © 1980- by Princeton University Press; *Logic*, ed. J. R. deJ. Jackson, copyright © 1981 by Princeton University Press; *Biographia Literaria*, ed. James Engell and Walter Jackson Bate, copyright © 1983 by Princeton University Press; and *Lectures 1808-1819: On Literature*, ed. R. A. Foakes, copyright © 1987 by Princeton University Press.

Finally, I thank my wife, Andrea, for her help, encouragement, and patience.

ABBREVIATIONS

AR   *Aids to Reflection.* Edited H. N. Coleridge. Bohn's Library. London: George Bell and Sons, 1890.

BL   *Biographia Literaria or Biographical Sketches of My Literary Life and Opinions.* 2 vols. Edited by James Engell and Walter Jackson Bate, Vol. 7 (1983) of *The Collected Works of Samuel Taylor Coleridge.* Edited by Kathleen Coburn and Bart Winer. 16 vols. Bollingen Series 75. Princeton: Princeton UP; Routledge and Kegan Paul, 1969-.

L&L   *Coleridge on Logic and Learning.* By Alice D. Snyder. New Haven: Yale UP, 1929.

CMC   *Coleridge's Miscellaneous Criticism.* Edited by Thomas Middleton Raysor. Cambridge, MA: Harvard UP, 1936.

CPW   *Coleridge: Poetical Works.* Edited by E. H. Coleridge (1912). New York: Oxford UP, 1969.

CSC   *Coleridge and the Seventeenth Century.* Edited by R. F. Brinkley. Durham: Duke UP, 1955.

CL   *The Collected Letters of Samuel Taylor Coleridge.* Edited by Earl Leslie Griggs. 6 vols. New York: Oxford UP, 1956-1971.

CN   *The Collected Notebooks of Samuel Taylor Coleridge.* Edited by Kathleen Coburn. 4 vols. Bollingen Series 50. Princeton: Princeton UP, 1957-.

CIS   *Confessions of An Inquiring Spirit.* Edited by Harold Bloom. New York: Chelsea House, 1983.

CS   *On the Constitution of the Church and State.* Edited by John Colmer. Vol. 10 (1976) of *The Collected Works.*

DHI   *The Dictionary of the History of Ideas: Studies of Selected Pivotal Ideas.* Edited by Philip P. Wiener. 5 vols. New York: Charles Scribner's Sons, 1973.

EOT   *Essays On His Own Times.* Edited by David V. Erdman. 3 vols. Vol. 3 (1978) of *The Collected Works.*

F	*The Friend.* Edited by Barbara E. Rooke. 2 vols. Vol. 4 (1969) of *The Collected Works.*
IS	*Inquiring Spirit.* Edited by Kathleen Coburn. London: Routledge and Kegan Paul, 1951.
LS	*Lay Sermons.* Edited by R. J. White. Vol. 6 (1972) of *The Collected Works.*
LoL	*Lectures 1808-1819: On Literature.* Edited by R. A. Foakes. 2 vols. Vol. 5 (1987) of *The Collected Works.*
L	*Lectures 1795: On Politics and Religion.* Edited by Lewis Patton and Peter Mann. Vol. 1 (1971) of *The Collected Works.*
LR	*The Literary Remains of Samuel Taylor Coleridge.* Edited by Henry Nelson Coleridge. 4 vols. London: William Pickering; New York: AMS Press, 1967.
Logic	*Logic.* Edited by J. R. deJ. Jackson. Vol. 13 (1981) of *The Collected Works.*
M	*Marginalia.* Edited by George Whalley. 5 vols. Vol. 12 (1980) of *The Collected Works.*
PL	*The Philosophical Lectures of Samuel Taylor Coleridge.* Edited by Kathleen Coburn. London: The Pilot Press; New York: The Philosophical Library, 1949.
TT	*Specimens of the Table Talk of the Late Samuel Taylor.* Edited by H. N. Coleridge. 2 vols. London: 1835.
TM	*Treatise on Method, as Published in the Encyclopedia Metropolitana.* Edited by Alice D. Snyder. London: Constable & Co., 1934.

PREFACE

I present this study to a broad audience, one including undergraduate students, specialists in Romanticism, and all those interested in nineteenth-century culture and thought. Conducive to this broad appeal is Coleridge's eclecticism and interdisciplinary approach to knowledge, for his theological interpretation of history encompasses politics, philosophy, literature, the natural and social sciences, Fine Arts, and other fields. This wide-ranging allusiveness is certainly the most interesting aspect of his thinking, especially as it relates to history.

Coleridge experimented with pivotal ideas, a fact evidenced by the later notebooks and letters which form the groundwork of the published texts. As a multidisciplinary thinker, he believed that knowledge could be harmoniously unified, and his work is virtually an education in the liberal arts and sciences.

More than just an erudite generalist with unorthodox study habits, Coleridge advanced a unified concept of human experience, generically identifiable with an entire tradition of writing, extending from the third century A.D. to the present. As a "theologian of history," he articulated a model for Western history conforming to the principles of Scholastic antecedents, upholding his political philosophy, and opposing desacralizing trends in Enlightenment and early nineteenth-century historical research.

Diffused throughout a multiplicity of texts, and discontinuously produced over nearly four decades, the historical thought has thus far eluded thorough analysis—the scholarship, to date, constituting an incisive yet fragmentary reflection of its subject. To remedy this, I have built upon the central idea that, for Coleridge, history can only be understood theologically. On this basis, I have organized, contextualized, and assessed his opinions.

C.D.
Staten Island, New York

CHAPTER ONE

Introduction

A review of the scholarship will indicate that the interrelationship between Coleridge's theological and historical thought has not received sufficient treatment.[1] If we were to view the historical thought as a dimension of his theology, it would then become clear that he composed a "theology of history," a genre placing human experience within the larger framework of Scriptural revelation. P. L. Hug defines this genre incisively, pointing out that this kind of historiography is a "branch of theology," assessing "the uniqueness and the universality of God's providential action in history, and the various phases of the divine plan."[2] Embracing all of human experience, as well as secular culture, such a record is a "salvation history," the meaning and purpose of which is derived from the Bible.

Adapting periodical schemes from classical and Jewish sources and using a two-fold format, Christian historians subdivided Western history according to important Scriptural events: a Jewish and a Christian era, corresponding to the Old and to the New Testament, respectively. From the Christian viewpoint, these dispensations related typologically: Old Testament prophecies are interpreted as foreshadowing New Testament persons, places, and events, all of which fulfill their prefigurations. Both prospective and retrospective, this dynamic scheme is subsumed under Divine Providence.

Adhering closely to the Biblical chronology, from Genesis to the Book of Revelation, Christian writers used important Biblical events, such as the Incarnation and the Resurrection, to demarcate history. In addition, orthodox exegetes, such as Sts. Paul and Augustine, maintained that Providence and the free will were coextensive and that the freest exercise of the will was to discern and to cooperate with God's Will.

Along with its universal scope, periodical and prefigurative structure, and providential direction, theological history was endowed with an eschatological dimension. According to Scriptural exegetes, salvation history culminated in a drama of the Last Things, fulfilling God's plan and mankind's purpose. The nature of this drama has been widely interpreted. Concepts such as "apocalypse," "millennium," and "*parousia*" appear frequently in the literature, but are often used imprecisely.

The term "apocalypse" needs special consideration since it figures so prominently in the works of both theological historians and Romantic writers. Derived from the Greek word "apokalyptein," which means "to uncover," the word "apocalypse" denotes, on the one hand, the prophetic enunciation of God's word. Yet, in a more mundane sense, "apocalypse" came to mean His extraordinary intervention into human affairs, usually through the cataclysmic levelling of the existing socio-political order and through its replacement by a heavenly kingdom. A thousand-year reign of God on earth preceding the Last Judgment and fulfilling prophecies made by St. John in Revelation, the millennium was considered a prelude to the Second Coming of Christ.

Crucial to Christian historians is a concomitant distinction. Theorists subscribing to the revelatory interpretation of "apocalypse" tended to expect a gradual disclosure of God's Will and, consequently, became more concerned with the life and history of the Church. Since God's design is inscrutable, they approached history faithfully, rather than speculatively. Thus "millennialists" revised the more dramatic "millenarian" perspective that, according to Norman Cohn, envisaged salvation as a collective, imminent, and terrestrial upheaval.[3]

Similar to the early Church Fathers who had expected Christ's imminent return and who therefore considered such a record superfluous, the idealistic historians of the later eighteenth and early nineteenth centuries (that is, the German idealists and the first-generation Romantics) were millenarianists who believed that the French Revolution was the apocalyptic fulfillment of Revelation.[4] In a sense, the early Fathers of the Church and the English Romantics faced a common dilemma: once the millenarian paradigm proved untenable, it was necessary to reformulate universal history.

This study documents Coleridge's theological solution to this problem. From 1798 to 1834, he constructed a millennial historiography supplanting the discredited, millenarian model. In this revised scheme, the Anglo-Saxon imperium displaced French republicanism as the focus of both political culture and eschatological history.

I will also establish the generic and dogmatic affinities of Coleridge's post-revolutionary historical thought to the traditional theology of history. After discussing Coleridge's poetic response to the Revolution and his reaction to the Enlightenment, primarily to Gibbon's *Decline and Fall of the Roman Empire*, I will focus on the most significant features of the genre, namely typology, providence, creation theory, universality, periodicity, and eschatology.

The greatest challenge of all has been to assemble, coherently, Coleridge's sometimes incomplete and discontinuous commentary. But with the guidance of Richard Haven and Laurence Lockridge who have outlined structural and historical methodologies for Coleridge studies, I have been able to consolidate the most important texts under specific headings and have then related Coleridge's thinking to his antecedents and contemporaries.[5]

Before beginning the generic analysis, I will provide some background to the history of theological history. Because this topic comprises hundreds of figures and works, an orientation chapter requires a careful and selective approach. So that we will have an accurate idea about Coleridge's place in this tradition, I will present the development of the genre in terms of four dialectically-contiguous phases, each of which turns on the question of whether or not sacred historiography has a place in the modern world.

CHAPTER TWO

The Development of Universal History

For nearly two millennia, the idea of sacralized history has been the subject of profound debate. Modern theologians have pointed out that the problem is to reconcile the historical to the eternal, a dialectical tension that from the times of the early Church has been a characteristic feature of Christian theology.[1]

In order to reconcile the idea of the historical Church to its transhistorical mission, Christian historians have enunciated two opposing interpretations. During the first or patristic phase of this debate, the first to the fourth century, the millenarian view obviated the need for a theological history recording the events of the early Church. Expecting Christ's imminent return, Christian exegetes devalued the significance of both the past and the present. In the second phase, extending from patristic to early modern times, the conventional theological and ecclesiastical history developed fully, deriving primarily from the seminal works of Augustine, Orosius, and Eusebius. The gravitation from a millenarian to a millennial perspective reflected the understanding that a literal apocalypse was not imminent. Consequently, historians turned their attention to the Church as an institution and community. With the coming of the modern age, broadly the period from c. 1400 to 1800, the emergence of national historiography and major developments in historical research during the German Enlightenment precipitated the desacralization of history. Coleridge's speculations are situated, therefore, at a very crucial juncture in the evolution of historiographical research.

1. History Truncated, the first to the fourth century

Their historical consciousness determined entirely by Scripture, early Christian chiliasts anticipated the Second Coming and what they believed was to be the consummation of historical time.[2] This viewpoint obviated universal history, for all that mattered was the bilateral structure of the Bible: the Old Testament prophets had foretold the Incarnation and Christ's redemptive mission, and the New Testament was a record of prophecies fulfilled. Preoccupied with the idea of an imminent *parousia*, patristic writers, such as Justin Martyr, Tertullian, and Hippolytus of Rome, searched the Bible for insights to the future. Referring especially to apocalyptic texts such as Daniel, Isaiah, Matthew, chapter 24, and Revelation, they concluded that a thousand-year period of spiritual and of material plenitude would precede the Second Coming and the Last Judgment. A sense of urgency also refrained through many Biblical texts. Matthew, chapter 24, was very popular in this regard because of its chiliastic warning of a "great tribulation" (24: 21), of "false prophets" (24: 24), and of signs in the heavens (24:29-30). Thus, concerned with the Last Things, the patristic writers turned away from things past and present.

Gradually realizing that they could not foresee the Second Coming and that changes had to be made to discern with more clarity God's Will in time, the Church Fathers deemed eschatological matters the province of faith, not of forecast. Turning to more temporal concerns, they began to document Church history, especially the idea of apostolic continuity and the notion that, until the fulfillment of time, the Church would remain a community faithful to God's Scriptural promise and open to His revelation. The moral urgency and anticipation of patristic exegesis gave way to more reflective and methodological approaches to theological history.

With this new emphasis on the social, political, and ecclesiastical history of the Church, Christian writers, especially Eusebius, Augustine, and Orosius, sought a means of correlating sacred to profane history; thus began a profound debate, the major issues of which preoccupy theologians today.

2. History Sacralized, fourth to the fifteenth century

Eusebius (263-339) has been called the "Father of Ecclesiastical History," an appositive justified primarily by his monumental, *History of the Church* (311-325), in which he reconstructed the earlier centuries of Christian history. Although he relied to a great extent on predecessors, and although he incorporated as much historical and apologetic material as possible, his purpose exceeded annalistic compilation, for he intended to write a theodicy, seeking, in G. A. Williamson's words, "to justify the ways of God to men," the final justification of which being "the overthrow of God's enemies and the triumph of the Church."[3] Reconsidering the relationship between sacred and profane matters, Eusebius's emphasis is unequivocal: "Any man who intends to commit to writing the record of the Church's history" must go right back to "Christ

Himself" (33); thus Constantine's great victory, in this providential light, evidenced divine favor.

Eusebius's historical endeavor provided Christianity with a temporal record. But, with the ascendancy of Constantine, a new problem had arisen: Christians began to identify the Roman Empire itself with God's Will. By endowing sacred history with an imperial dimension, they blurred the distinction between Church and State. Many important Christian writers promulgated this controversial idea, failing to realize how ahistorical and problematic it was to identify a regime as divinely favored. They also failed to see that such a view contracted to the limited historical scope of the patristic writers.

The danger was experienced first-hand in 410 A.D. when the Christian Visigoths sacked Rome. After eight-hundred years of assumed invulnerability, "Eternal" Rome had been vanquished. There were recriminations; pagans blamed Christians for Rome's decline and fall and rejected the idea that the Roman Empire had a significant role to play in history.

Acutely aware of the consequences arising from the concatenation of sacred and profane history, Augustine re-defined the character and historical purpose of the Church. In *Concerning the City of God Against the Pagans*, he distinguished between Two Cities—the City of God and the Earthly City—purporting that the world could only know these two communities in an intermixed, rather than a pure, state.[4] Since the City of God could not exist on earth, the Christian historian had to approach temporal events circumspectly, for neither meaning nor stability could be assured by the Earthly City. Augustine does not deny that, like the Roman Empire upon which God had bestowed much favor, temporal kingdoms can and do play important roles in the divine plan; however, once these roles were completed, he asserts, temporal kingdoms would vanish. For this reason, theology and the imperium should not be confused.

The paradox of Augustine's achievement is that, in order to conserve the primacy of sacred history, he had to limit the importance of ecclesiastical and of imperial history. However, Orosius, whom Augustine enjoined to write a theological history, could not accept the latter's dissociation of the Two Cities.[5] Through historical examples, Augustine had urged Orosius to show that Christians had not caused the fall of Rome. But, because he saw a direct succession from Christ to Augustus, and because he believed that Christianity sanctified the Roman Empire indelibly, Orosius, in his *Seven Books of Histories Against the Pagans*, linked God's plan with temporal history. For a periodical model, he turned to the Book of Daniel. Orosius revised Daniel's four monarchies or empires

(Babylonians, Medes, Persians, and Macedonians) to make room for Rome: the Babylonian, Macedonian, Carthaginian, and Roman.[6] For Orosius, as well as for St. Jerome, the fourth and most protracted period was the Roman phase in its Christian form, a period essential to the fulfillment of sacred history. Diverging sharply from Augustine's binary model, and arguing that from his times to the Last Judgment world history was in its final, Roman phase, Orosius re-unified the Two Cities.

Variously and circumstantially interpreted, the problem of the Two Cities, either in its unitary or binary form, would shape later responses to universal history. Hindsight would vindicate for medieval and early-modern theologians of history the correctness of Augustine's view. By 500 A.D., the Roman Empire would merge with the German world when the Germans invaded. The urgency of Orosius's task was renewed: it was necessary to re-define the character of the Two Cities. With respect to the German invasions, much rationalizing would occur, some proposing that God was punishing Rome, others that He was converting the Germans surreptitiously. Some of these speculations were perspicuous, for the Germanic invasions did indeed unify German and Latin culture under the Roman Church, an eventuality many perceived as an act of divine favor.

Eusebius, Augustine, and Orosius enunciated and debated ideas that would influence medieval historiography profoundly. Accelerating our survey over six or seven centuries, we can see that most prominent medieval works, such as Otto of Friesing's *The Two Cities: A Chronicle of Universal History in the Year 1146* (pub. 1157), emulated patristic forerunners. The institutional Church is once again equated with sacred history; in the case of Joachim of Fiore's work, for example, apocalyptic pronouncements abound. But, when we reach the early-modern period, the patristic format would undergo significant changes.

3. History De-Sacralized, c. 1400-1800

From c. 1400 to 1800, complex events, such as humanist text criticism, a revival of interest in pagan literature, geographical expansion, the Reformation, and the development of the new science, contributed to the decline of theological history.[7] The debate over sacred and profane history would continue, however, with post-Reformation historians tending, generally, to align themselves with Augustine. But the movement of historical theory was, irreversibly, towards secular universal history and towards the substitution of concepts such as rationalism and human freedom for God's immanent will.

Historical thinkers of the early Enlightenment based their political theories on empirical psychology and on the need for verifiable data.[8] For them, history proved an inexact enterprise; its composition and verifiability relied too much on memory, and it did not qualify as a legitimate science. The popularity of the idea of progress, and the realization that nature could not be used as a standard for human conduct, contributed to the modern conception of human history. For many, rationalism and the imperative of human freedom, doctrines of faith transcending the incompleteness of nature and the mutability of human life, would become cohesive historical principles.

In the works of Vico, Montesquieu, Voltaire, Gibbon, Herder, Turgot, Condorcet, and others, the goal of history is identified with the conquest of nature and with the realization of a secularized city of God, the groundwork of which was Reason. This rational teleology provided a humanistic standard by which to measure and to guide historical institutions and, thus, mankind's progress. To the French revolutionaries and to Anglo-German enthusiasts, especially the first-generation Romantics, this sense of rational progress exceeded the realm of social and political reformation, taking the form of secular millenarianism and revolution. Obsessed with the vision of a rational State and with their perceived mission to institutionalize it at all costs, the French revolutionaries attempted to redress social inequities, but they did so chiliastically, zealously justifying violent revolution as a necessary evil, and levelling the old order to establish a rational society based on liberty, equality, and fraternity. Instead of universal justice and the fulfillment of a global democratic process, however, the French Revolution devolved into tyranny, terror, and warfare.

A more thorough revaluation of the historical relationship between nature and freedom was needed, and this was undertaken by German Idealists, such as Hegel, who tried to reconcile the imperatives of natural law and human freedom with consciousness and reason; for the idealist, history became an inscrutable, immanent, and dialectical process, moving towards human freedom and coinciding with mankind's rational nature.

Despite the secularization of historical thought from the Enlightenment to the first half of the nineteenth century, and despite the proliferation of theories, it would be incorrect to assume that the traditional sacred history had been entirely eclipsed. Bossuet's *Discourse on Universal History* (1681), contrary to what some scholars have said, was not the last attempt to construct a traditional theological history.[9] His *Discourse* is unquestionably traditional: the past is divided into six millennia; the

Incarnation is the focus of history; there are seven world ages; and the Last Judgment is the consummation of time. Bossuet's recrudescence of the genre combined Augustinian and Orosian features, but his identification of French monarchs as modern heirs to the Roman Empire indicates, beyond a doubt, that he favored Orosius's approach.

Bossuet's resistance to the de-sacralization of universal history—for many of this age, a natural consequence in the development of historical scholarship—provoked Voltaire to advance a purely-secularized version of history in his *Essay on the Manners and Spirit of Nations* (1744). He asserted that history was anything but fortuitous, being "little else than a long succession of useless cruelties."[10] Evidently, whatever the individual motivation or strategy, historical thinkers could no longer be satisfied with inflexible paradigms, inherited from patristic and medieval antecedents.

4. The Germanic Context, 1780-1825

Works such as Vico's *New Science* exemplify the eighteenth-century inclination not so much to supplant God from human affairs, but rather to explain the complexities and paradoxes of world history more adequately. Seemingly-inexplicable events such as earthquakes, warfare, and famine, which seemed to belie the concept of a benevolent cosmology, had to be accounted for.

Remanding Providence to the shadowy background of human concerns, and seeking that which was most factually demonstrable, German theorists at the turn of the century made major advances in historical scholarship. Before we can understand Coleridge's relationship to the Germans, it is necessary to distinguish between two groups of German historiographers whose approaches differed markedly from one another.[11]

As philosophers of history, the *Universalgeschichten* moved away from the traditional, Scripturally-oriented framework and, in some instances, substantially reduced the theological format. In works such as Kant's "Conjectural Origin of the History of Mankind" (1785) or Schiller's "Something Concerning the First Human Society, according to the Guidance of the Mosaic Record" (1790), the Biblical narrative of the Fall and of redemption, though not invalidated as in the works of Voltaire and Gibbon, was nonetheless translated into secular terms. Herder, Kant, Schiller, Fichte, Schelling, and Hegel (who followed Lessing) also wrote universal histories which were essentially secularized versions of the Christian paradigm.

Schelling's conjectural history in his *System of Transcendental Idealism* (1800) illustrates this secular gravitation.[12] He periodizes Western history into three parts: periods of Fate, of Nature, and of Foresight. The first is a kind of Golden Age, the greatness and nobility of which can be inferred from archeological evidence. During this period, presumably comprising Mesopotamia, Egypt, and ancient Greece, there prevailed a primitive spirituality Schelling calls "Fate" (it is unclear if he means Greek "moira"), apprehended then as an impersonal "ruling power" that "frigidly and unconsciously destroys even the most glorious things." The concept of Fate, in the next contiguous period, "reveals" itself as "Nature." The primitive conception of Fate, at about the time of the early Roman republics, was conceptualized and "transformed into an explicit law of nature." This is an immanent teleology which "forces freedom and unrestrained arbitrariness to serve a plan of nature," gradually introducing "a mechanistic lawfulness into history." Though abstract, impersonal, and imperious, Schelling's law of nature differs from his concept of "Fate": natural laws disclose phenomenal design and purpose. Despite the deterministic tendency of these historical laws, they operate, constructively, to further the civilizing impulse that extends from nation to nation: "Unconsciously and even against their will [the nations] were forced to serve a plan of nature which, in its complete development, must bring about the all-inclusive league of peoples, the universal state." Schelling's rational progressivism exemplifies the glaring deficiencies of teleological history, especially in the way that civilizations are reduced to ciphers: all of the events of this period, even the most momentous such as the decline and fall of Rome, are merely "natural results," bereft of suffering and of moral content, and serving only to unify Western civilization.

"Foresight" will prevail in the third period. With prospective understanding, the entire continuum of history will be apprehended, and what the ancients conceived to be the dominions of "Fate" and "Nature" will be revealed as necessary aspects of an all-encompassing theodicy. By 1800, in view of the failure of the Revolution, Schelling is understandably cautious about proclaiming his epoch a prophetic junction. But he does assert that "when this period comes, then God himself will be."

The teleological, periodic, and apocalyptic (in the revelatory, not revolutionary, sense) aspects of Schelling's outline, along with the modernist bias (the present moment is the cognitive and social apex of a progressive development) were inherited from the original tradition of theological history. Most important is the secular focus: the source of historical knowledge is shifted from the mind of God either to the mind of man or to a dialectical relationship between the human mind and an impersonalized, rational archetype, which is objectified as informing history, as determining events, and as unfolding over millennia. Schelling's immutable, rational immanence—which reveals itself gradually and only when the time is ripe—is a substitute for Divine Providence. Although this rational abstraction is reputed to have constructive effects and a socially-unifying purpose, it differs radically from the orthodox conception of God. In fact, Schelling explicitly supplants God's omnipotence and omnipresence with this abstraction, reducing the divine ontology to the level of finite progression; hence, God's existence in the world, according to Schelling, is incomplete and will only be realized once the prophetic age occurs; thus the immanence of God, in Schelling's formulation, is contingent upon mankind's prescience, a heresy from most orthodox viewpoints. Schelling's rationalized eschatology retains the structural conventions of the traditional genre—periodicity, apocalypticism, teleology, and universality—but intentionally disengages from both Biblical design and orthodox dogma. This secular transvaluation, which Coleridge uniformly rejected, identifies Schelling's conjectures, and the works of the *Universalgeschichten* generally, as collateral to the orthodox tradition.

Schooled in the tradition of theological history like their idealistic counterparts, theorists at the Universities of Göttingen and of Berlin also confined their historical writings to a Biblical framework.[13] But, as they developed their research skills, and since they sought cultural relativity, these thinkers began to consider the preconceived Biblical format as vestigial; however, they were equally dissatisfied with the speculations of the idealists who failed to reconstruct the past quantitatively. Thus, critical of the philosophers' secular idealism, the German philologists or "higher" critics, favored a more empirical approach to historical studies. From c. 1760 to 1830, philological historians—e.g., Gatterer, Schlözer, Niebuhr, and Müller—were designing "general" histories, empirical counterparts to the *Universalgeschichte*. Ironically, although many of the philologists faulted the philosophers for expounding speculative designs, and although the former made a practice of substituting tangible data for abstractions, the philologists left intact the Biblical design of early history. Gatterer and Schlözer, for instance, calculated epochs in reference to Scriptural events, such as Creation, the Flood, and the Incarnation. Despite their orthodoxy, they, too, moved in the direction of analytical research.

Pursuing analytical content and critical depth, the philologists were understandably dissatisfied with English universal history. As leaders in the field, the English had been producing a monumental world history: *An universal history from the earliest account of time*... (London, 1736-1765). Because this thirty-eight volume project had been yielding discursive and unannotated works, the Göttingen professors broke with the English example to produce a series of popular histories appealing to the general reader. Gatterer, for one, produced eight unique versions of universal history. The first epoch-making edition provided an unprecedented quantity of cultural history, widening the horizon on the field, and achieving a measure of organic unity. Called "the father of universal history," Schlözer carried the project further in 1769, by rejecting the notion of a co-operative work (with one expert writing on France, another on Venice, and so on), and by maintaining that world history had to be adequately differentiated from serialized history, as well as from speculative philosophy. The purpose of universal history, he reasoned, was to show how the earth and humanity as a whole came to the state in which it now stood and to demonstrate how all phenomena reflected the workings of an immanent historical principle. The greatest innovations in universal history during this period were yet to come with the work of Leopold von Ranke.

Particularly in his *Histories of the Latin and Germanic Nations from 1494 to 1514* (1824), Ranke, the head of the "scientific" school at the University of Berlin, sought to reconcile philosophical idealism with philological research.[14] Though he believed that religion was the key to history, he was not a traditional sacred historian: his theism was grounded on an effort to interconnect historical events in larger patterns; historical data, he asserted, had to derive from careful analysis, not from preconceived ideals. Though he advocated a hermeneutical approach, Ranke still tried to formulate an idealistic universal history. In so doing, he faced an inherent contradiction. He makes it clear that the "supreme law" governing his research is the "strict presentation of facts," attained through the study of "memoirs, diaries, letters, diplomatic reports, and original narratives of eyewitnesses." Yet, at the same time, he wished to conserve the idealistic component of his work: "the historian must keep his eye on the Universal aspect of things."[15] The problem he faced was: how can one reject aprioristic historiography—that is, one reputedly having "no preconceived ideas"—and hope to reconcile the two approaches? He reiterates, in a fragment from the 1860s, that the pursuit of "synthetic" history is an ideal goal, but that universal historiography must be inclusive and comprehensive, comprising "a solidly rooted understanding of the entire history of man" anchored in critical research. Historical writers must work in two directions simultaneously: "the investigation of the effective factors in historical events and the understanding of the universal relationship." The translation of theory into practice, however, would prove problematic for Ranke, for Coleridge, and for an entire generation of historical writers.

Precisely how Coleridge approached the problem will be detailed in the chapters to follow. At this crucial juncture in the development of the philosophy of history, his work can be described as a reaction to the secularizing propensities of the Enlightenment, as a recrudescence of the sacred paradigm inherited from the apostolic Fathers, and as a correlative to, rather than a derivative of, German idealistic theory.

CHAPTER THREE

The Chiliastic Verse

Coleridge's earliest speculations on theological history and related themes are found in the poetry of c. 1794-1800. There he considers the French Revolution to be the apocalyptic fulfillment of the Book of Revelation. Gradually, as events to the contrary unfolded, he became disillusioned with this eschatological prospect. Republican terrorism and hegemony, reactionary oppression in England, European absolutism, war with France, and the 1798 French invasion of neutral Switzerland forced him to recant his belief in the Revolution as the focus of providential history. Consequently, he turned from a vatic perspective in "Religious Musings" to more circumspect analyses of current events in "Ode to the Departing Year" and "France: An Ode," hoping, there, to understand the disjunction between contemporary history and the theodicean paradigm. Upon this understanding, he hoped to reconstruct his theological history.

Because these themes were so complex, Coleridge, from about 1800 on, would explore the problems of history and politics, not in poetry, but in discursive prose. These early poems are nonetheless significant because they show that, during the revolutionary crisis, he was trying to understand, philosophically, why the millenarian structure collapsed. Like the patristic writers, he realized that reading God's Word into even the most extraordinary events was an inexact and hazardous enterprise. Hindsight would reveal that the French betrayal of principle and the English reaction, which together had precipitated his crisis of faith, were actually part of his education as a theological historian. Sobered by historical reality, he moved from bitterness and ambivalence to a more analytical and cautious perspective. His Christianity deepened, though he radically emended his interpretation of how God worked in human affairs.

Coleridge's richly eclectic and exhortative poem, "Religious Musings" (1794; pub. 1796), assimilates contemporary political history into an eschatological framework.[1] Teleologically conceived, all of the evils of recent history—this "sea of blood bestrewed with wrecks" and these "mad / Embattling Interests" (*CPW* 124-6)—are transient conditions necessary to the fulfillment of a providential design. This optimism is reflected in the Argument to the poem: "the present State of Society"—i.e., the terrorist phase of the Revolution and the First Coalition against France ("the thirsty brood of War" [170])—reputedly evidences God's divine plan, prefigured in the prophetic books of the Bible. Influenced also by Newton, Hartley, Priestley, and others, whose design arguments he would reject a decade later for their mechanically-contrived features, Coleridge makes the crucial point that history subserves theology and that all events were divinely regulated by "The Supreme Fair sole operant: in whose sight / Alike from all educing perfect good" (56-8).

Once it became incontrovertible that the Revolution had devolved into tyranny, Coleridge tried to revise his theodicy. In "Ode on the Departing Year" (1796), he considers the relationship between tyranny and the millenarian premise, the fast-fading assumption that the Revolution heralded a new heaven and a new earth. This was, undoubtedly, a difficult task for the enthusiast, in view of the September Massacres (Sept. 2-3, 1792), the execution of Louis XVI (Jan. 21, 1793), France's declaration of war on England (Feb. 1, 1793), and the Reign of Terror (1793-1794), events dramatizing the widening disparity between the preconceived design and contemporary history. Confused and ambivalent, Coleridge eventually abandoned the millenarian pulpit, acridly forecasting the retributive punishment of reactionary England.

In the first retrospect of the poem, Coleridge focuses on recent French history, 1789-1796. Behind a screen of personified abstractions masking a heartfelt desire for social equity is a voice now sternly censoring the republicans who, in the name of Liberty, had "let slip the storm, and woke the brood of Hell" (34). An 1803 note identifies "The Name of Liberty... at the commencement of the French Revolution both [as] the occasion and the pretext of unnumbered crimes and horrors," as Coleridge reiterates his disdain for Pitt, for European absolutists, and for the French republicans.

Gradually, Coleridge understood that there was little distinction between absolutist and republican tyranny. In the second retrospect, he impugns Catherine the Great (1729-1796), on November 17th, the anniversary of her death; he then defames her authoritarianism and attacks Russian hegemony in Poland and Turkey (38-61). While surveying Russian policy, 1762 to 1796, the speaker, in an 1803 note, summarily denounces Russian feudalism and the "Northern Conqueress" (40 and n.). Catherine's anti-republicanism, he believed, was actually a symptom of her moral depravity which he illustrates, biographically, with the murder, in June 1762, of Czar Peter III, and politically, with reference to her intransigent absolutism during the Peasant Uprising (1773-1775).[2] To regicide, adultery, and domestic oppression, Coleridge adds three decades of imperialism, implied by the allusion to "Warsaw's plain" (47). This refers to Catherine's Polish hegemony. By placing her former lover, Stanislaus Poniatowski, on the Polish throne in 1764 as Stanislaus II, Catherine established a virtual protectorate over Poland. Coleridge then turns to the subsequent partitioning of Poland by Russia, Prussia, and Austria, which had inspired Kosciusko's short-lived rebellion. And, in the third retrospect, he cites Russian expansionism during the Russo-Turkish Wars, and especially General Suvarov's (1729-1800) brutality at the Massacre of Ismail (Dec. 22, 1789), where a Turkish garrison and town population were decimated (162n.). For Coleridge, Russian imperialism represented the kind of tyranny republicanism was expected to remedy.

The fourth retrospect examines the British slave trade, 1619 to 1796. "Afric's wrongs, / Strange, horrible and foul!" (88-9), the slave trade constituted, for Coleridge, a flagrant, governmentally-sanctioned abrogation of human dignity. In his 1796 "Lecture on the Slave Trade," he asks the rhetorical question: "is it possible that they who really believe and fear the Father should fearlessly authorise the oppression of his children! the Slavery and tortures, and dreadful murders of tens of thousands of his Children[?]" (*L 1795* 245). He also indicts British imperial policy in India, as well as the practice of scalping during the American War, and reinforces this survey with a note, transposed from the 1795 "Addresses to the People," on Flanders and La Vendée (165-66n.). Perplexed by the widespread evil of recent times, yearning for some evidence of theodicy, and momentarily encouraged by the French Constitution of 1795, the speaker exhorts the "Spirit of Nature" to hasten the apocalypse ("O rise and deal the blow!" [99]). Despite this record of atrocities, he continues to affirm that Divine Providence regulates "all the events of time, however calamitous some of them may appear to mortals" (Argument, p. 160).

Although grateful to Providence for having spared England from invasion, Coleridge nonetheless fears that her international policy will eventually incur divine retribution; thus he envisions his country's "predestin'd ruins" (147). Then, turning his "immortal mind" from the prospect of a socially-transfigured earth and from the brink of national catastrophe, he seeks spiritual renewal, finding "In the deep Sabbath of meek self-content" (159) a spiritual refuge where he might be cleansed of "fears" and "anguish" (159-60n.).

Coleridge realizes, in "Ode on the Departing Year," that in their imperial propensity absolutist and republican regimes share a dark kinship. He also understands that spiritual and moral solutions could not be found in the reactionary climate at home. Under these conditions, he had to modify his theodicean perspective.

Narrowing his temporal scope to the revolutionary decade, 1789-1798, Coleridge, in "France: An Ode," reviews his political life and hopes. His disillusionment stemmed from what Professor Carl Woodring describes as "an intellectual dissatisfaction with the materialism and empiricism of Hartley and Priestley, and with all the doctrines appropriated by the French," as well as from "a deep spiritual thirst not satisfied by doctrines of natural rights and reform."[3] With the 1798 French invasion of neutral Switzerland, the divergence of contemporary political history from the theodicean format became incontestable. He responded to these events, in "France: An Ode," by recanting his revolutionary enthusiasm and by converting political concepts into metaphors of the mind in relationship with nature.[4] A momentary liberation from ideology, "France: An Ode" represents his most searching exploration of political evil.

Re-surveying the revolutionary years—1789 to 1795, from the "Declaration of the Rights of Man and Citizen" (August 4, 1789) to the declaration of war on England (Feb. 1, 1793) (22-42)—and the events responsible for his crisis of faith, Coleridge explains that, although he "defended revolutionary ideals," he still loved his country, weeping "at Britain's name" (41-45). He relates how the mounting evidence of French intentions had forced him to revise his views and how the post-Thermidorean period (July 1794 to the end of Oct. 1795) revived his hope in the light of the Directory's new Constitution.

His hopes oscillated from 1789 to 1795—i.e., from revolutionary expectation, to a rejection of republican terror, to the hiatus of the Directory—and then progressed to a fourth stage, 1795 to 1798, at which he repudiated France as "adulterous" and "blind." In the fifth verse-paragraph, he comes to a significant conclusion: for the "sensual and the Dark" (85), "Liberty," in its fullest sense, was virtually unattainable without spiritual reformation. Large-scale social change, it follows, depended cumulatively upon the moral character of each individual.

The collapse of millenarianism, documented in "France: An Ode," should not suggest that Coleridge had abandoned theodicean speculations altogether or that he had become completely skeptical about the possibility of discerning a City of God. His faith was immeasurably deeper than the confessional tenor of these poems might suggest. But he had still to understand the Voltairean view that history was nothing more than a struggle for power. Fundamentally, the question Coleridge asked himself was whether the idea of an historical theodicy could be viably maintained in such uncertain times. By 1808, he would re-explore the idea of history, but this time in discursive prose.

CHAPTER FOUR

Reaction Against the Enlightenment: The "Canonization" of Edward Gibbon

The medieval heritage of historical writing, exemplified by Bossuet's *Discourse on Universal History* (1681), flourished well into the eighteenth century, but it did not go unchallenged. Professing to study history according to a scientific ideal, *philosophes*, such as Gibbon, Hume, and Robertson, rejected medieval historiography in favor of a new relativism.[1] Although, as in Voltaire, a strong polemical voice is heard, the *philosophes* still raised important questions about historical causation which could not be answered within the inflexible confines of sacred history. And, although they did not combine with this pragmatism the pursuit of an overriding explanation for historical change, their efforts re-directed the discipline. By de-sacralizing historical writing, they paved the way for the kind of exacting research done by the German philologists whose work differentiated history from theology and widened the ethnographic perspective on world history.

Coleridge's reaction to Gibbon is an index of his opinions on Enlightenment historiography. Surprisingly, his anticipated defense of sacred history, and especially of early Christianity in the context of the Roman Empire, is tempered by a genuine respect for Gibbon's talents. Though his work on Gibbon's *Decline and Fall* is discontinuous and fragmentary, it can still be assembled and positioned in the ongoing scholarly debate called "The Gibbon Controversy," which had begun with eighteenth-century reactions to Gibbon's historiography in Cambridge and Oxford, and which has continued to the present day.[2] Despite its disorganization and ideological undercurrents, Coleridge's work constitutes a hitherto unacknowledged contribution to this inquiry, one evidencing his serious commitment to historical studies.

Consisting of a dozen fragments of varying length, the majority of which are notebook entries, letters, recorded conversations, and marginalia, Coleridge's opinions on Gibbon can be subdivided into two parts. The first contains direct and indirect praise for Gibbon who is described either as an eloquent, industrious, and erudite writer, or as one whose work Coleridge uses as an authoritative background to his own speculations. Comprising attacks against Gibbon's style, rhetoric, and methodology, the second is more extensive and explicit. Before reviewing Coleridge's criticism, however, it is necessary to differentiate his philosophical position from that of Gibbon.

Northrup Frye has pointed out that Gibbon not only intended to provide a faithful account of the later Roman Empire, but also to distinguish between "the reality of what was happening to Rome, as he saw it, and the illusions, whether pagan or Christian, that the Romans themselves held about their place in history."[3] It was Gibbon's secondary intention—to de-sacralize Christianity—that would precipitate most of the adverse reaction to the work. Coleridge's orthodox conviction that an authentic universal history was necessarily a *Heilsgeschichte*, or sacred history, led him to reject Enlightenment historiography, especially the works of the philosophers who, as Peter Gay has observed, "made their revolution in history by secularizing its subject matter."[4] Specifically, Coleridge rejected Gibbon's thesis that Christianity was part of the barbaric invasion that had destroyed ancient culture and that had introduced the Dark Ages. On the contrary, Kathleen Coburn tells us, Coleridge argued that Greek and Roman culture had actually died of "intellectual inanition and the social decadence that was at once part cause and part result of it" (*PL* 43). In keeping with his orthodoxy is his conviction that the advent of Christianity had actually synthesized the best features of Hebrew, of Greek, and of Roman culture, fulfilling the providentially-ordained development of Western civilization—a view Gibbon had lamented as "the triumph of barbarism and religion" (*D&F* 1:865).

In light of such sharp differences on the historical significance of Christianity, it is surprising to see that Coleridge credited Gibbon for his range and meticulousness. In the midst of accumulating indictments, commendatory remarks will suddenly appear. One such mixed indictment can be found in Note 3824 (May 1810). After assailing him, Coleridge adds that Gibbon, "with all these faults is still our greatest Historian ... he's to be canonized" (*CN* 3:3824). The allusion to "canonization" ironically derides Gibbon's antagonism towards Christianity and particularly his deliberate downplaying of the Roman persecutions of the Christians (*D&F* 1:444-505).

In other contexts, Coleridge was less ambivalent about Gibbon's talents. The laudatory phrase of 1812, "eloquent historian" (*EOT* 2:352-53), becomes a superlative in 1819 when he calls Gibbon "our most eloquent historian" (*PL* 181-82), and expresses his "highest respect for the learning, the industry, and the genius of Mr. Gibbon" (*PL* 229). Although balancing this with several deprecatory clauses ("but he had no philosophy; and he never fully understood the principle upon which the best of the old historians wrote" [*TT* 264]), Coleridge, in 1833, reiterates this sentiment and respect for Gibbon's "immense learning" (*TT* 15; *PL* 421-22; *IS* 181-82).

If not for Coleridge's repeated reliance on Gibbon's scholarship either to back his own arguments or, ironically, to attack Gibbon himself, these encomia might be too readily dismissed as empty flattery. The praise, however, was authentic, and yet part of Coleridge's strategy to defend Christianity. One instance of how Coleridge used Gibbon's scholarship as a critical weapon against him occurs in a 1795 lecture. Here, Coleridge challenges anti-Christian, Roman accounts, drawing source material from Paley and Gibbon, and then directs his fire at Gibbon's thesis about the rapid spread of Christianity (*L 1795* 169-71; *D&F* 1:382-444).

There are other instances of indebtedness. As early as April, 1795, Coleridge had studied *The Decline and Fall* for background material to a prospective lecture, "On the Rise, Progress and Decline of the Roman Empire" (*L 1795* xxxiv). Although this lecture never materialized, he continued to study Gibbon's Rome, an interest culminating in a 1798 article entitled "Rome." Borrowing liberally (and, at times, inaccurately) from Gibbon, Coleridge lamented the record of the foreign occupation of Rome, beginning with Alaric and continuing with Napoleon in 1796-97 (*EOT* 1:25-26n.). Occasional references in the 1802 essay series, "Comparison of France with Rome" (*EOT* 1:311-39), suggest that there, too, Gibbon's history was a primary source. Similarly, the background source for "Buonaparte and the Emperor Julian" is none other than "our greatest historian," whose authority is caustically re-enlisted against Napoleon. Undoubtedly, Coleridge believed that Gibbon was a competent scholar upon whose work his own speculations might be based.

From 1818 to 1833, Coleridge was writing sporadically, though insightfully, about the rules of good writing. Along the way, he made some comments about the cultural implications of Gibbon's style: that his artificial style reflected a general decline in morals. In his 1818 essay "On Style," Coleridge defines good prose as being appropriate, perspicuous, and not easily translatable, and he alludes to a variety of excellent writers: Bacon, Milton, and Taylor (*LoL* 2:237, 233). Historically, the most interesting dimension of his discussion concerns the causative relationship he discerned between the spirit of a given age and its prevailing prose style. Pre-Restoration writers, for example, were in themselves, as he continues in "On Style," "the great patterns or integers of English style," for each used a unique idiom. Writers such as Milton were to be admired, therefore, for writing with stately "gravity." But, after the Glorious Revolution, contends Coleridge, English prose style became artificial, reflecting poor public taste, a decline in morality, and the rise of the commercial spirit (234-37). Gibbon's style is especially affected and rhetorically self-conscious: it is "the worst of all," having "every fault of which this peculiar style is capable" (237). Although not fully developed, Coleridge's observations on the relationship between language and culture are evocative. No doubt, in his view, Gibbon's alleged affectation, indirection, and pomposity illustrate the thesis that a despiritualized culture produced an artificial prose style. The logical question is: did Coleridge apply to specific texts the criteria of propriety, of perspicuity, and of untranslatability, and arrive at some coherent deductions about language, culture, and Gibbon's purposes?

Unfortunately, Coleridge's analysis is sporadic. In an 1810 Note on this topic, for instance, he had substituted enumeration for close textual analysis. In this particular note, he urges tutors to inform their students about the reputed shortcomings of Gibbon's style: his monotonous and effeminate periods—his overuse of complex sentences in the passive voice—his frequent use of indirection, of periphrasis, and of circumlocution, and his absurd use of the conditional verb "might." Worst of all, he claims, is Gibbon's putative avoidance of lively idiomatic expressions, for which he substitutes "pompous enigmatic jargon," as well as indefinite language generally (*CN* 2:3823). The limitations of this Note are enlightening: Coleridge's castigation of Gibbon's artificial and unethical style was intended less for Gibbon the writer, whom he repeatedly described as "elegant," than for Gibbon the propagandist. In other words, Coleridge seems more concerned with how Gibbon applied his literary skills.

Coleridge's 1810 commentary has a definite place in the Controversy. Gibbon's contemporaries had criticized his style from several standpoints. The anonymous critic of *The Analytical Review*, for example, advanced the untenable argument that Gibbon was stylistically inept. Others, the majority, in fact, faulted Gibbon for using his rhetorical and stylistical skill as a propagandistic vehicle. H. E. Davis, in his *Examination* (1778), charges that, to cover misrepresentation and deceit, Gibbon had employed beautiful language, especially in chapters fifteen and sixteen of *The Decline and Fall*. And Joseph White, in his 1784 Bampton Lectures, censures Gibbon for using stylistic elegance to make popular the licentious opinion about the Five Causes of Rome's fall.[5] The apparent contradiction in Coleridge's critique—that Gibbon's style was both "elegant" and "detestable"—is easily resolved once one sees that, following precedents set by White and others, Coleridge was most likely concerned with how and why Gibbon used style to promulgate an anti-Christian position.

Gibbon's critical methodology is the topic of conversation in an 1833 *Table Talk* item. The problem with this critique—a text that would evoke the hostility of J. M. Robertson (1907), of G. M. Young (1933), and of S. T. McCloy (1933)—is its tone and discursiveness.[6] Neither illustrating nor documenting his contentions, Coleridge simply lists Gibbon's rhetorical weaknesses, faulting him for providing rhetorical sketches, rather than substantive analyses, of key personages and events; for being anecdotal; for sacrificing psychological analysis to scenic effect; for ignoring details and less prominent factors generally; for focusing on what was traditionally, not critically, noteworthy; for portraying figures in an inflated or distorted manner, and, in effect, detaching them from their respective milieux (thus they seem, in Coleridge's words, to "come and go"); and, most strikingly, for employing an artificial mode of construction (chronology), hindering any serious inquiry into the nature of historical causality.

Since Coleridge failed to develop and to document his ideas, it is difficult to trace his remarks to contemporary sources. It can be logically assumed, however, that he was aware of the literature and of the major arguments propounded for and against Gibbon. In fact, there is ample precedent for much that Coleridge says—ironically, Gibbon's own admissions in his *Autobiography*.[7]

In the remaining documents—several passages in *The Statesman's Manual* (1816), portions of the seventh *Philosophical Lecture* (1819), and a marginalium (c. 1825) on Jeremy Taylor's *Liberty of Prophesying* (1647)—I have tried to compensate for Coleridge's chronic discursiveness by being as systematic as possible, reading each as an eclectic construct having a unifying pattern and concern and, it is to be hoped, a larger intellectual context. The focus of the passage in *The Statesman's Manual* is philosophical: Coleridge objects to the rational underpinnings of eighteenth-century historical writing—that is, to Lockean empiricism and to Humean skepticism, both of which influenced Gibbon.[8] He makes a crucial distinction between theological and "mechanical" historiography:

> The histories and political economy of the present and preceding century partake in the general contagion of its mechanical philosophy, and are the product [Copy G: Artifacts] of an unenlivened generalizing Understanding. In the Scriptures they are the living educts [Copy G: Produce; Copy R: Growth] of the Imagination; of that reconciliatory and mediatory power,

which incorporating the Reason in Images of the Sense, and organizing (as it were) the flux of the Senses by the permanence and self-circling energies of the Reason, gives birth to a system of symbols, harmonious in themselves, and consubstantial with the truths, of which they are the conductors.
(*LS* 28-9)

Differentiating the rational from the Scriptural perspective, Coleridge expresses his conviction that history should be read as a *Heilsgeschichte,* an authentic, Biblically-oriented account of mankind's temporal relationship with God. According to this definition, any historical account extraneous to this providential matrix would be fragmentary, at best—one temporal aspect of an all-encompassing teleology—while any secular history claiming universality exclusive of, or contrary to, Biblical authority would be counterfeit.

Coleridge believed that this sense of incompleteness and of inauthenticity was inherent both in Gibbon's derivative method and chronological organization. Though having no real doubts about Gibbon's stylistic ability, he did fault the structure of *The Decline and Fall* for being a well-sewn patchwork of noted classical sources, such as *The Historia Augustus* or Dion Cassius's *History of Rome* (*D&F* 3:881-84). Gibbon was well aware of this. Ironically, comments in his *Autobiography* support Coleridge's later allegations. Discussing the shortcomings of the accretive method, for example, Gibbon speaks of how, as a young man influenced by Lockean precepts, he had relied primarily on three sources for his research on Rome and of how this reliance seriously limited his scope. Thus, in the "infancy" of his reason, he recalls how he had uncritically digested in "a large commonplace book" material from Pascal's *Provincial Letters,* from Abbé de la Bleterie's *The Life of Julian,* and from Giannone's *Civil History of Naples* (24-6). Retrospectively, Gibbon admits how inexpedient this practice had proven to be. But Coleridge implies that Gibbon never truly relinquished this method: that, in adulthood, he continued to practice it in a more sophisticated and purposeful manner. Because this method was reputedly at work throughout *The Decline and Fall,* he concludes that Gibbon's historical range was inherently limited and a pale counterpart to the kind of universal history contained in the Bible.

Accusing Gibbon of having offended "against the most serious duties of an historian" ostensibly concerned with historical causation, Coleridge, in 1819, questioned his sense of decorum. He outlines, but fails to develop, what he considered elements crucial to a comprehensive historical method: 1) the veracity of causes; 2) a proportional emphasis upon these causes; 3) inclusiveness; and 4) the contextual evaluation of these causes. The emphases upon veracity, proportionality, inclusiveness, and contextuality appear to comprise a sensible method, unintentionally recalling Hume's rhetorical question: "What would become of history, had we not a dependence on the veracity of the historian according to the experience which we have had of mankind?"[9] But Coleridge's objections were motivated, mainly, by his need to defend sacred history against Gibbon's attack. With this purpose in mind, Coleridge challenged Gibbon's specific assertions that early Christian millenarianism actually accelerated the conversionary process;[10] that New Testament prophecies of the Destruction of Jerusalem were questionable; and that Christianity contributed to the decline of Rome (*PL* 229-35). Arguing, conversely, that as part of God's plan the decline of Rome actually fostered the unity of Western Christendom, Coleridge concentrated on the third point. Because, in his view, *The Decline and Fall* amounted to a chronicle, he maintained, in 1833, that Gibbon failed to grasp the actual cause of Rome's decline and fall which he reputed to be the "imperial character overlaying and destroying the national character" (*PL* 421-22).

The most substantive treatment of this subject can be found in his marginalium on Jeremy Taylor's *Liberty of Prophesying*. Igniting a critical debate that has continued to the present, Gibbon postulated "four principal causes of the ruin of Rome, which continued to operate in a period of more than a thousand years": the injuries of time and nature; the hostile attacks of the barbarians and the Christians; the use and abuse of material resources; and the domestic quarrels of the Romans themselves (*D&F* 3:863ff.). Motivated mainly by religious indignation, the bulk of the eighteenth- and nineteenth-century criticism focused almost exclusively upon Gibbon's Five Causes for the progress of Christianity, none of which were affirmed as being providential (*D&F* 3:383). Elucidating a number of interrelated religious, demographic, strategic, political, and economic forces that they believe had contributed to the fall of Rome, modern critics, many of whom have dissociated the theological from the secular content of the issue, have focused upon and have augmented Gibbon's Four Causes outlined in chapter seventy-one.[11]

Despite the brevity of his comments, a fault he acknowledged (*LR* 2:278), Coleridge attempted to integrate the Four Causes of Rome's decline and fall with the Five Causes of Christianity's rise to prominence. His thesis is that the decline of Rome and the concomitant rise of Christianity were interdependent socio-cultural phenomena: the gradual disintegration of the Empire—due largely to military despotism and to overextended colonial borders—predisposed it to the establishment of Christianity. What I call Coleridge's "Two Causes," both of which

Gibbon had treated to some extent, had led eventually to the "extinction of patriotism," as well as to "the melting down of states and nations in the one vast heterogeneous Empire" (*LR* 2:276). Gibbon had cited the long peace (which caused intellectual sterility), economic exploitation (which made most Romans unwilling to defend what they did not own), the lack of freedom, and a sprawling, indefensible Empire.[12] For Coleridge, the gradual disintegration of Roman culture and civilization had created a religious vacuum in the colonial Empire, producing "in thousands a tendency to, and a craving after, an internal religion." From this teleological viewpoint, Coleridge believed that the decline of Rome and the rise of Christianity were anything but fortuitous: "the necessity of religion, and the untenable nature and obsolete superannuated character of all the others, occasioned the conversion of the largest though not the worthiest part of the newly-made Christians."

More Orosian than Augustinian, Coleridge's theological interpretation of Roman history certainly differentiates his view from that of most Enlightenment thinkers. From his universal perspective, he calls the advent of Christianity "the most stupendous of miracles," Divine Providence having predisposed the "events by which the whole world of human history, from north to south, east to west, directed their march to one central point, the establishment of Christianity" (*LR* 2:277-78).

Coleridge's work in the Gibbon Controversy is erudite, for he was familiar with the literature; however, his originality is difficult to assess conclusively because the topics he addresses, such as the Five Causes or the life of St. Athanasius, were commonplace. The question of originality notwithstanding, Coleridge's diversified approach to Gibbon is significant and, in the aggregate, more substantial than some have recognized. And, despite its dogmatic nature, his work contains a measure of objectivity in the form of genuine praise for Gibbon's scholarship and style. Coleridge's major objection is directed to how these talents were used. Occasional indiscretions of tone (exaggerated by critics) do not subvert his eclecticism.

Coleridge's resistance to Gibbon's historiography is a preamble to my analysis of his reconstructive work, which shall begin with his use of the typological method of comprehending human experience.

CHAPTER FIVE

"A Wonderful Accordance": The Figural Method

Coleridge formulated a coherent historical scheme incorporating secular experience into the sacred framework. To demonstrate the conviction that history was a theodicy, he interpreted Scripture typologically or figurally, the use of this method identifying him, unequivocally, as a theological historian. J. Robert Barth has observed that, even though Coleridge did not always distinguish clearly between this and other senses of Biblical interpretation, he used this method and understood the dangers inherent in its misuse.[1] The typological method was integral to his understanding of history as a redemptive drama.

Letters and notebook entries, particularly from 1825-1827, indicate that Coleridge read history theologically and had planned a full-scale universal history. A prospectus for historical studies in the "Opus Maximum" manuscripts, for example, is subdivided into six parts, beginning with Genesis and extending throughout Biblical history. Established upon "the superior Authority and Historical Reliability of the Hebrew Origines Gentium," this project would have culminated with an ecclesiastical history, "the Philosophy, and philosophic Abstract of the History of the Visible Church & Christendom from the Apostles to the present time" (*L&L* 3-8).

Like the Fathers of the Church, Coleridge understood that the interests of Church and State had to be balanced carefully, and that each field of interest was vital to the other. Though he believed that the theological content of history was, morally, the more significant of the two, he also understood that revelation and the idea of a theodicy were unintelligible unless historically contextualized. Thus, in a balanced and dogmatic system, he strove to interrelate theology and world history. Notebook entries, 1825 to 1833, convey this integrative effort. In one entry, he states that, the "History of Christians ... cannot be rendered intelligible, without the History of Men, or general History" (*CN* 4:5304). As an historical institution and system of belief, Christianity, he asserts in another context, endows world history with meaning and hope: "But for Christianity: Christendom, as center of convergence," he writes in 1833, "I would utterly want the *historic* sense."[2]

Coleridge reiterates the idea that history is the matrix of Christianity, and that the two are dialectically interrelated: "HISTORY ... under its highest form of Moral freedom, is that *alone* in which the Idea of Christianity can be realized" (*CN* 4:5300). He delineates this dialectical construct in the first letter of his "Confessions of an Inquiring Spirit": his creed, or system of *credenda* begins with God, "The Absolute ... in whose transcendant I AM, as the Ground, *is* whatever *verily* is:—The Triune God, by whose Word and Spirit, as the transcendant Cause, *exists* whatever *substantially* exists" (*CIS* 40). From this Trinitarian position, he recounts mankind's spiritual history from the Fall, to the Resurrection, to the liturgical life of the Church. To reconcile secular to salvation history, he adapted from the *Naturphilosophen* the concept of polarity:

> Christianity is fact no less than truth. It is spiritual, yet so as to be historical; and between these two poles there must likewise be a midpoint, in which the historical and the spiritual meet. Christianity must have its history—an history of its introduction, its spread, and its outward becoming; and, as the midpoint above-mentioned, a portion of these facts must be miraculous, that is, *phaenomena* in nature that are beyond nature. Furthermore, the history of all historical nations must in some sense be its history;—in other words, all history must be providential, and this providence, a preparation, and looking forward to Christ.
> (40-41)

Arguing for the spiritual vitality of ecclesiastical institutions, Coleridge considered the Church, not the State or its National Church, to be a sacramental construct embodying God's providential Will. Yet both sacred and secular history were subsumed under Providence, constituting a living prologue to the *parousia*. The temporal record of the Church was also spiritually significant. It was an eschatological prolegomenon, an incarnation "looking forward to Christ."

These observations suggest that Coleridge read history prophetically, employing the figural or typological method of interpretation. This sense of Biblical interpretation, J. Robert Barth maintains, "involves the reference of a person, object, or event in Scripture prophetically to some other person, object, or event, as, for example, Adam is seen not only in terms of his immediate role in Genesis but also as a type or figure of Christ (Rom. 5:14)."[3] Joseph A. Mazzeo's incisive description of this method is also helpful:

> The kind of historiography we find in Scripture is ... prophetic, and the method of understanding it can be called figural or typological interpreta-

tion. Persons and events become the bearers of meanings, figures of another order of reality, transcendental in meaning but lying on the axis of time. This view establishes an ontological relationship between two persons or events such that the first is not simply itself in its own proper significance but also signifies the second which comes after it. The second implies, refers to, or fulfills the first. They are related as shadow to image ... as types of each other or as type to antitype. The two elements of a figure are separated on the temporal axis but they lie along it. They are both real persons or real events and are incorporated into temporality and the flow of history. They are therefore real and only our grasp of their deep and real interconnectedness is an act of the inspired mind. The interconnectedness is not ordinarily perceived by the skeptic for it is not a causal interconnection but rather flows from the relation of both elements of such a figure to Divine Providence which both ordains the history of salvation and bestows on man the means of comprehending it. The link between both ends of such an analogy or real metaphor is provided by God, who permits us to see the resemblance through the structures of revelation.[4]

Understood typologically, therefore, a prophecy and its fulfillment—e.g., Isaiah's prophecy of the Suffering Servant (53:3-12) and its fulfillment in Christ's Passion more than seven-hundred years later—transcend temporal and cultural contexts, constituting a new ontological reality and evidence of God's historical immanence. To a degree, the typological method permits the faithful exegete to apprehend the concept of God's eternal present, what Boethius (c. 480-524) had eloquently phrased, "*interminabilis vitae tota simul et perfecta possessio*" ("eternal life possessed perfectly and simultaneously").[5]

Employing the typological method, Coleridge conceived of human history as a theodicy. Since Scripture presents "the stream of time continuous as Life and a symbol of Eternity," the contemplation of Biblical events, especially in the prophetic relationship between the Old and New Testaments, disclosed the idea of the *tota simul*, the simultaneous totality of divine existence or God's eternal present in which "the Past and the Future are virtually contained in the present" (*LS* 29-30). For Coleridge, the temporal designations of "Past" and "Present" are subsumed, ontologically, under God's eternal Presence. Hence, sacred history—history read according to the Bible—encompassed the secular past and was, at once, prospective or "prophetic" and retrospective or "historical."

In a series of important letters, Coleridge used organic metaphors to describe the inner workings of salvation history. In the first letter of this series (June 6, 1826; to J. H. Frere), he considers the "Historic *Idea*" as a duality successfully maintaining the integrity of natural causation and the free will:

> The Historic *Idea* is the same in Natural History (Physiogony) as in History, commonly so called—but polarized, or presented in opposite & correspondent forms, [the] purpose of the latter is to exhibit the moral Necessity of the Whole in the freedom of the component parts: the resulting Chain [being] necessary, each particular link remaining free. (Our old chroniclers and Annalists satisfy the latter of the requisition; Hume, Robertson, Gibbon, the former half; in Herodotus, and the Hebrew Records, alone are both united.) In the History of Nature the same elements exist in reverse order.—The absolute Freedom, WILL both in the form of Reason . . . and [its] own right as the Ground of Reason . . . is the Principle of the Whole in the necessity of the component Parts.
> (*CL* 6:583)

Informing human history, Coleridge postulates, is a "moral Necessity" or "Chain" of pre-determined events, implicitly evidencing the governance of Divine Providence. Temporal phenomena—each "component part" or "particular link"—remain freely determined within the providential context.

Coleridge elaborates on the internal mechanism of sacred history in a second letter (May 25, 1827; to H. F. Cary):

> Organization is either simultaneous as in [an] individual animal, or successive—as in one of Handel's or Mozart's Overtures. Now in every scheme of Organization Successive (and the great scheme of Revelation is eminently such) every integral part is of necessity both prophecy & history, save the last or consummating Fact, which will be only History, and the initial which can only be prophecy: but of all the intervening Components of the Scheme every part is both at once—i.e. Prophecy in relation to what follows and History in relation to that which had preceded.—Now in this sense of the word I believe the whole Bible to be prophetic . . . .
> (*CL* 6:684-685)

An anterior enunciation becomes "historically" significant once it is fulfilled, at which moment both phenomena—the prophecy and that which is prophesied—generate an ontological reality, both historical and transcendent. To the faithful exegete, this discloses God's timeless presence and presence in time. In this reconciliation of opposites, *kairos* subsumes, but does not obliterate, *kronos*.

Aware of the importance of ordinary phenomena, Coleridge explains that events intervening between the prophecy and its actualization not only contribute to its fulfillment, but are also absolutely necessary to this consummation: they are providentially ordained to partake in, and to contribute to, the inexorable fulfillment of the prefigured event. Understood in this sense, intervening phenomena are symbols (*LS* 30), sacramental tropes, explains J. Robert Barth, through which God communicates Himself to, and shares His power with, mankind.[6] Because the intervening events subsist in, and are causally-related to, the fulfillment of a particular prophecy, they consequently enact God's Will, unfolding temporally as consubstantial phenomena. Scriptural reality—each person, event, place, and thing—exists unalterably in accordance with God's immanent Will while the individual will remains sacrosanct and inviolable. Transplanted from natural to theological history, the concept of "Organization Successive" provided Coleridge with a way of describing the dynamics of sacred history.

Trying to assimilate "a magnificent Scheme of *History* a priori" into a closed temporal system, one extending from Creation to the Last Judgment, Coleridge, in the third letter of this series (June 2, 1827; to H. F. Cary), continued to apply organic metaphors to his orthodox scheme. He conveys his sense of an immanent teleology figuratively, applying to his sacred history the phylogenetic hierarchies of naturalists such as Linnaeus or Blumenbach, and thus exemplifying the kind of analogical writing popular to eighteenth-century scientific discourse:[7]

> ... the whole chain of Predictions from Adam to St. Paul, given to Man in the five forms, necessary to the full manifestation of the Manhood [of the Race], 1. The Individual—2. the *Kind* or Universal—3. The Races—4. The Family. 5. [The] Nation—to be such as could only proceed from a *special extraordinary* influence of the Holy Spirit—and that you agree with me in the remaining sense. It is scarcely possible that any one should estimate either the prophetic Spirit or the particular prophecies of the Bible, at a higher value than I do, as feeding, strengthening, deepening, and enlarging the faith of a Believer. The mistake is in the using them, as the foundation-stones of the Edifice, instead of [its] Pillars—in beginning from them with Infidels, a[s] PROOFS of an Argument, the very Data of which suppose the Belief that is to be produced by it. The right use of the Prophecies is to regard them, as a magnificent Scheme of *History* a priori containing the Class, the Orders of the class, and the Genera of the Orders, with the corresponding classic, Ordinal, and Generic Characters—which are found realized in them .... I see all past History provided for in the Scheme: and I do not, say rather I cannot doubt, that the Future will be found equally correspondent as soon as the number of particular Events shall be sufficient to form & fill up the next Epoch: for no Prophecy is of *private*, i.e. individual Interpretation. And for this reason is every Prophecy instructive of the true meaning, the essential character and import of the Events, in which they are fulfilled. The Prophetic Word is the Light of the Present ....
> (*CL* 6: 689-690)

Informing human history, the Divine Will is envisaged as a reticulating, self-organizing process. Reiterating a notion from the letter of May 25, 1827, Coleridge speculates that prophecies disclose the Divine ordonnance (or taxonomy) of history. Divine Providence, though selective, is phenomenologically inclusive: non-prophesied or ancillary events—"the series of actual Events" or "Individua"—will, in turn, be "collated" with the prefigurations into "a wonderful Accordance." In addition, phenomena will literally "arrange themselves into species that occur in the very sequency of the distinguishing Characters which are found realized in them" (*CL* 6: 689-90). Consequently, mundane events will contribute to, and partake in, the larger leavening design, for temporal phenomena are informed, *ab initio*, by God's Will.

Although Coleridge's conjectures on the dynamics of figural history are presented informally and discontinuously, their significance is undiminished. Not only do these speculations reflect great erudition, but they also demonstrate the generic affinity of his thinking to the traditional sacred history: human history is a theodicy, the course of which can be discerned through the contemplation of Scripture. Distinguishing Coleridge's figural interpretation from those of his predecessors is his recurrent practice of using contemporary theory, such as German organic metaphors, to describe and to modernize the traditional paradigm. Relative to Coleridge, these theories and concepts represented the best in natural philosophy.

The use of the figural method presupposes the belief in an all-encompassing Providence, a doctrine also involving the question of free will: how can the volition be free in a foreordained context of events? Influenced by many Christian thinkers—especially Sts. Paul and Augustine and the seventeenth-century English Divines—Coleridge resolved this antinomy. This orthodox solution further demonstrates the theological orientation of his historical thought.

CHAPTER SIX

"The Great Drama of the World": The Idea of Providence

On the question of Providence, which entails the antinomy of Divine foreknowledge and the free will, the evidence indicates that Coleridge was a theological "reconciliationist" in the heritage of Sts. Paul, Augustine, and Thomas, and the seventeenth-century English Divines.[1] Unlike predestinarians, such as Calvin and his successors, whom he refuted, and unlike determinists and philosophical reconciliationists from Hume to Kant, Coleridge, as J. Robert Barth, S.J. points out, subscribed to the belief that God's foreknowledge, though absolute, did not preclude the free will, for Coleridge adopted an Augustinian conception of historical freedom: "there can be no contradiction between man's freedom and God's free election, because man's perfect freedom is the conformity of his finite will with the Absolute Will of God."[2]

Although his commentary on St. Augustine is sparse, Coleridge's position on the antinomy of the free will appears congruent, nonetheless, to that expressed in *The City of God*, where Augustine argued for the coextension of Providence and free choice: "[W]e are in no way compelled either to preserve God's prescience by abolishing our free will, or to safeguard our free will be denying (blasphemously) the divine foreknowledge. We embrace both truths, and acknowledge them in faith and sincerity, the one for a right belief, the other for a right life."[3] Coleridge might have found a more direct source of Augustinian doctrine in Boethius's *Consolation of Philosophy* (see *BL* 2:121). Boethius recapitulates Augustine's view:

> ... what God sees as happening must necessarily happen; but in the case of things freely chosen by men the necessity is found only in God's knowledge of the event, not in the nature of the event itself. All things will happen which God knows will happen, but some of them will happen as a result of man's free will. Nor is God's knowledge changed by our changes of mind. Providence anticipates every future action and sees immediately what seems to us a succession of choices and actions. The freedom of the human will is inviolate and imposes upon men a grave obligation to act virtuously, for all their actions are done in the sight of the Judge who sees all things and rewards and punishes according to his perfect knowledge.[4]

Another principal source for Coleridge's speculations on Divine Providence is St. Paul. Speaking of the "restless cravings" and discontents of his times, Coleridge urges that history be studied holistically, a perspective from which ethical truths might be discerned. Thus, from "the collation of the present with the past," from the thoughtful assimilation of the "events of our own age to those of the time before us," an historical inquirer might derive moral lessons applicable to contemporary life. Of particular importance, in this regard, are the extraordinary events of Scripture:

> ... it would be inconsistent even with the *name* believers not to recur with preeminent interest to events and revolutions, the records of which are so much distinguished from all other history by their especial manifestation of divine interference. 'Whatsoever things,' saith Saint Paul (Romans xv. 4.) 'were written aforetime, were written for our learning; that we through patience and comfort of the Scriptures might have hope.'
> (*LS* 9)

Coleridge refers to St. Paul as one who rightfully extolled the edifying purpose of Biblical history. Citing other Pauline texts—Colossians 1: 26-7, 2: 2-3 and Ephesians 3: 16, 18—as prolegomena to meditations on the gradual revelation of Divine Truth, he returns to the "philosophic Apostle of the Gentiles":

> For all things are but parts and forms of its progressive manifestation, and every new knowledge but a new organ of sense and insight into this one all-inclusive Verity, which, still dilates it to capacity of yet other and yet greater Truths and thus makes the soul feel its poverty by the very amplitude of its present, and the immensity of its reversionary, wealth.
> (*LS* 179)

The wealth of Divine revelation, he suggests, is accrued through moral choice that, if consonant with the Absolute Will of God, will confer freedom, thereby allowing a person to share in God's plenitude. In other words, God's eternal presence can be comprehended through the free participation of the creature with his or her Creator. Thus, writes Coleridge:

> The elements of necessity and free-will are reconciled in the higher powers of an omnipresent Providence, that pre-destinates the whole in the moral freedom of the integral parts. Of this the Bible never suffers us to lose sight. The root is never detached from the ground. It is God everywhere: and all creatures conform to his decrees, the righteous by performance of the Law, the disobedient by the sufferance of the penalty.
> (*LS* 31-2)

Concentrating on the workings of Providence in universal history, Coleridge, in his *Philosophical Lectures* (1819), interprets the course of Western civilization as the collective development of human consciousness under divine guidance; history is, therefore, the "striving of a single mind," from Jewish monotheism, through intermediate stages of pagan idolatry and of polytheism, to Christianity (67). When surveying the history of philosophy, he observes that, "the mind is beforehand impressed with a belief of a providence guiding this great drama of the world to its conclusion" (87). Western history had moved, inexorably, towards the establishment of Christianity: Providence was universally active, and "the whole march of human affairs" was directed to this fulfillment (170-1). Furthermore, it has been "the intention of Providence," he affirms, "from the ancient Roman empire" to modern times, to "diverge the rays that are to enlighten and civilize the rest of the planet" (254). His Protestant interpretation of history convinced him, too, that the Reformation manifested the beneficent "mark of Providence" (284).

The most comprehensive exposition of the neo-Pauline idea of Providence occurs in *Aids to Reflection* (1825) and in marginalia on the seventeenth-century English Divines (December 1825). Contending that "the man makes the motive, and not the motive the man," he poses the evocative question (thus paraphrased): how does the Divine Will preserve free choice (150)? He reasons that the natural order presupposes an antecedent unity, necessarily "present to all and in all, yet in no wise excluding or suspending the individual law or principle of union in each" (151). Envisioning the concept of the *tota simul*, he describes Creation as "one universal presence, a one present to the mind of God and as containing within itself a multiplicity of particulars" (151).

In *Biographia Literaria* (1817), Coleridge reiterates that human history is the means through which God reveals Himself and conveys His Will:

> For there is always a consolatory feeling that accompanies the sense of a proportion between antecedents and consequents. The Sense of Before and After becomes both intelligible and intellectual when, and *only* when, we contemplate the succession in the relations of Cause and Effect, which like the two poles of the magnet manifest the being and unity of the one power by relative opposites, and give, as it were, a substratum of permanence, of identity, and therefore of reality, to the shadowy flux of Time: and the perception and acknowledgement of the proportionality and appropriateness of the Present to the Past, prove to the afflicted Soul, that it has not yet been deprived of the sight of God, that it can still recognize the effective presence of a Father, though through a darkened glass and a turbid atmosphere, though of a Father that is chastising it ....(2: 234)

This is certainly an eclectic passage. Much of the rhetoric is adapted from necessitarian philosophy ("the relations of Cause and Effect"), and the polarity image recurs as a way of describing eternal revelation. But by far the most seminal sources are Pauline texts. When he refers to "the afflicted soul" yearning for the Beatific vision, for example, he is paraphrasing Corinthians 13: 2, "For now we see through a glass, darkly; but then face to face: now I know in part; but then I shall know even as I am known."

Coleridge's theistic resolution is grounded on the eighth chapter of St. Paul's Epistle to the Romans, specifically on the theme of mankind's divine inheritance and on the distinction between the undeserving person endowed with "the first fruits of the Spirit" (Romans 8: 23), while all of Creation "groaneth and travaileth in pain" (8: 22). Like St. Paul, he stresses humanity's spiritual legacy and absolute reliance on God's redemptive grace. Instead of abrogating the free will, Divine Providence communes with, enlightens, and regenerates the soul, for the Spirit of God, as St. Paul says in Romans 8: 26, acts on the individual will "by a predisposing influence from without ... though in a spiritual manner, and without suspending or destroying its freedom" (*AR* 214). As a limited and fallible creature (153-4), a human being can only be certain of his or her inherently-spiritual nature, an endowment elevating the person above nature or "the forms of time and space" (154).

Recognizing that the idea of predestination can also be inferred from the fact that a person relies upon God's omnipotence (*AR* 214), Coleridge reconsiders the theological problem posed by the doctrine of Election, cautioning his readers not to be confused by Calvinistic determinism. To avoid confusion, one should see a human being's relationship to God as an ongoing communion, the outcome of which is unknown to the individual but foreknown to God. Under such conditions, a Christian should understand the idea of Election, contingently and provisionally: it is "a hope" springing out of "Christian principles," one that should be examined in the light of revelation, "by the tests and nourished by the means prescribed in Scripture" (214). Because of human limitations, one can only "hope" for a greater assurance of salvation, since one's limited understanding of the redemptive process cannot "in this life pass into knowledge, much less certainty of foreknowledge" (214). The fact that one cannot be certain of one's own redemption makes it a moral responsibility though still a matter of free choice to discern God's Will and to act according to Divine Law. Only through an active Christian life, thought Coleridge, might an individual attain a measure of "lively" and of "assured" hope in salvation.

Closely related to his orthodox tract, *Aids to Reflection*, are December 1825 marginalia on the seventeenth-century English Divines. Commenting on Richard Field's (1561-1616) denial of free will in man, Coleridge distinguishes between the Absolute Will of God, subsuming each individual will, and the individual will itself, endowed by God with inviolable self-determination (*CSC* 160-1). Of the predestinarians' rejection of the free will, he writes, in a marginalium on Bunyan's *Pilgrim's Progress*, that their sophistry "rests on the false notion of eternity as a sort of time antecedent to time. It is timeless, present with and in all times" (*CSC* 483). Understanding the patristic and medieval distinction between *kronos* and *kairos*, a distinction the Calvinists confused, he rejects the kind of deterministic logic that reads: if a person's fate were foreknown and invariably fixed, then the spiritual efforts of the individual, such as contrition and penance, are entirely futile. A person's limited perspective, the inability to see as God sees, requires that he or she evaluate the progress of the soul, not in terms of presuppositions, but rather in terms of a gradually-unfolding Divine Will and of an unresolved personal destiny. On these grounds, he declares, "Those who persevere, will persevere, and God foresees" (*CSC* 483). To discern the Will of God, a believer has to be seriously committed to Christianity and to recognize that any doctrine claiming to obviate this commitment, by offering an alternative spiritual route, is inherently self-delusive. For Coleridge, God's sovereignty and man's freedom were inherently compatible.[5]

Coleridge reiterates this neo-Pauline idea discontinuously from 1826 to 1831. Though needing elaboration, the passages to follow demonstrate the doctrinal consistency of his thinking with respect to Providence. In a letter to his brother George (Feb. 8, 1826), he differentiates the idea of self-determination from that entertained by the pantheist who "determine[s] that Nature is *all*." On the contrary, self-determination elevates the human being above Creation, a fact that is self-evident:

> I am a self-determining Agent to the extent, that my Conscience makes me a responsible one—Therefore, I am not altogether a Link determined wholly by the Chain, with which I cohere: and I instance the reality of my Will in and by the free act of determining to believe the contrary. Why?—Because it is sufficient proof of its truth for an honest man.
> (*CL* 5:565)

Coleridge treats the orthodox view of Providence intermittently. In a Jan. 2, 1827 note, he writes that, "Man was made to know that a finite free Agent could not stand by the coincidence & independent harmony of a separate Will with the Will of God. Only by the Will of God can he obey

God's Will" (*CSC* 497). The interrelationship between individual free will and historical Providence recurs in *Church and State*: "the idea of moral freedom" becomes "the ground of our proper responsibility"; for "the *idea* of man's moral freedom possesses and modifies [one's] whole practical being" (17-18). Understood within a larger, providential context, the idea of inviolable freedom is revealed through "the science of History,—History studied in the light of philosophy, as the great drama of an ever-unfolding Providence"(32).

The typological interpretation of Scripture and the idea of Providence endow Coleridge's theological history with dynamic unity. Though diffusive, his opinions are still remarkably intelligent and eclectic, further demonstrating how seriously he thought about history during the post-revolutionary years.

In the three chapters to follow, I will present Coleridge's periodical scheme: his tripartite subdivision of world history into ancient and classical, early-modern, and modern periods. And I will highlight the almost inevitable shortcomings of such a preconceived history.

CHAPTER SEVEN

"Of Union and Ennoblement": Ancient and Classical History

Throughout the eighteenth century, the study of the past had been subordinated to, and restricted by, theology, philology, and law.[1] Gradually, with the increasing interest in the scientific treatment of historical data, historians began to handle documentary sources critically. In the University of Göttingen, especially, critics such as Mosheim, Semler, and Michaelis were treating the Bible as a philological and historical text, while others were doing the same with classical Greek texts. Ancient and classical scholarship, by the turn of the century, was clearly moving in a direction away from the inherited tradition of sacred history that regarded the Bible as the primary source for understanding the past.

Coleridge's work on ancient and classical history adheres to the sacred format inherited from scholastic and medieval sources. Dating from the reputed moment of Creation and extending to the Middle Ages, a span of forty-five centuries, the first epoch in his tripartite design comprises five Western cultures: the Jewish, the Greek, the Roman, the Celtic, and the Gothic. Reacting against secular historiography, and contrary to the analytical achievements at Göttingen, Coleridge reasserted the validity of Biblical history, with national cultures as subordinate aspects of this revelatory and redemptive drama; consequently, a given civilization was important only insofar as it contributed to God's plan for establishing Christianity. There were inevitable pitfalls to this preconceived approach. In this modified Augustinian format, for instance, dogma preempts not only cultural relativity, but also the possibility of ethnographic and regional analysis.

Although his treatment of ancient and classical history reflects an antipathy for the kind of approach Gibbon used, and although inherently restrictive and quite different from voluminous works such as B. G. Niebuhr's *History of Rome* (3 vols., 1811-1832; English trans., 1828-1842), Coleridge's work in this area is important in its own right. Largely overlooked, it is an essential aspect of his historical scheme.

Since his commentary is concentrated in the brief period from January 1818 to February 1819, existing mainly in the form of drafts, notes, lecture transcripts, and ancillary material, some care is required to reconstruct his ideas accurately and to relate them to the milieu. Such an assessment would be impossible, therefore, without some background in the history of science. Because his universal history begins with the origins of mankind, Coleridge was naturally concerned with the Genesis story of Creation. As a nineteenth-century sacred historian well-read in contemporary scientific theory, he tried to modernize the Genesis account through the appropriation of German ideas and conventions. Though, by modern standards, unscientific and at odds with pre-Darwinian breakthroughs, Coleridge's efforts were not atypical to the then-contemporary climate of intellectual accommodation and of metascientific speculation.

1. Natural History and Theological Accommodation, seventeenth to early nineteenth century

Seventeenth-century theorists correlated natural history to Scripture, and especially to the Book of Genesis.[2] Sacred historians—such as Ralph Cudworth (1617-1688), Henry More (1614-1687), and the Cambridge Platonists—speculated about the age of the earth and about the very time of Creation. A popular example of this sort of exegesis, surviving well into the nineteenth century, is Archbishop James Ussher's calculation, in 1654, that the earth had been created in the year 4004 B.C. Thomas Burnet's full-scale rendition of Biblical naturalism, in his *Theory of the Earth* (1681-1689), is another example of this kind of writing. Burnet's natural theodicy, which Coleridge would describe as "a grand Miltonic Romance" (*CSC* 492), ranges from paradise, through the Flood, to redemption, and accounts for geological processes within the parameters of the Fall and of redemption.

Natural philosophers of the eighteenth century published many books that attempted to place natural history into a theistic context. The purpose of the new science, in this light, was to reveal God's majesty in the world.[3] Works such as Nehemeiah Grew's *Sacred Cosmology*, John Ray's *The wisdom of God manifested in the works of the creation* (1704) and George Cheyne's *Philosophical principles of religion natural and revealed* (1705) were examples of the genre. Probably the most famous work of the period was William Derham's *Physico-theology* (1713), a title that became synonymous with this kind of reconciliatory approach.

Though the metascience of Ussher and Burnet persisted well into the late eighteenth and early nineteenth century, its credibility was gradually undermined by advances in paleontology and geology. In this regard, I would like to consider the ways in which two opposing geological schools of the eighteenth century, Catastrophism and Uniformitarianism, treated received doctrine.[4]

Ascribing geological features to intermittent cataclysms, the Catastrophes, like the earlier physico-theologians, tried to preserve the idea of special creation. One of its leading exponents, Abraham Werner, in 1775, modified Burnet's theory of a subterranean ocean in order to account for the presence of diversified fossils in geological strata. Werner's Neptunist theory, as it came to be called, was devised so as not to contradict the Bible: the Noachian deluge, he stated, was the last in a series of such events. Thus Catastrophism represented a compromise between the Mosaic account and the expanding geological knowledge of the period.

At the turn of the century, Catastrophes continued assimilating scientific evidence into the Biblical account. Baron Georges Cuvier (1769-1832), in his *Research in Fossil Bones* (1811; English trans., 1817), introduced Werner's theories to England and maintained the primacy of Scripture. Scientific researchers and writers such as William Smith (1769-1839), and later William Buckland (1784-1856), William Conybeare (1784-1857), and the German philosophers of nature, continued to frame their scientific conjectures with the Bible.

The major exponent of Uniformitarianism, James Hutton (1726-1797), proposed an interpretation of geological process undermining the doctrine of special creation, the Flood, and the notion of God's extraordinary intervention in natural history. Though he did not deny the existence of God, Hutton ignored the Flood hypothesis in his comprehensive study of physical geology. Fundamentally opposed to Catastrophism, Hutton's Uniformitarian theory held that the earth was a dynamic, self-regulating engine, governed by inherently-impersonal laws, and extending incalculably into the past. He presented his findings, in 1788, to the Edinburgh Philosophical Society, eventually publishing his work under the title, *Theory of the Earth with Proofs and Illustrations* (1795). Another famous Uniformitarian, Charles Lyell (1797-1875), vindicated Hutton's hypothesis, adumbrating ideas salient to Darwinian theory. Within this context, Coleridge would grapple with the problem of natural origins and human prehistory.

2. The 1828 Marginalium on Blumenbach and Note 4378

In light of these theories, Coleridge's speculations on the origins of the human race can best be described as accommodative: like the Catastrophes, he tried to assimilate modern scientific conjectures into the sacred format, with the intention of using science to corroborate theology. For scientific theory, he turned to the German philosophers of his day. As Trevor Levere has shown, Coleridge's interest in geology developed through his reading of natural philosophers, such as Lorenz Oken (1779-1851) and Heinrich Steffens (1773-1845), as he attempted to formulate "the principles of a philosophical cosmogony and geogony."[5]

When encountering ideas contradicting the moral and theological groundwork of his theodicy, however, Coleridge began to revise his estimation of German theory. Hence, from 1815 to 1819, he adopted and modified their models to suit his own cosmogony; by 1817, observes Levere, he would reject the theological implications of Schelling's and Steffen's schemes entirely. Unlike the Germans, he retained the book of Genesis as "the principal text organizing his philosophical cosmogony."[6]

When he tried to account for the origin and development of the human race, Coleridge also turned to German polarity doctrine, specifically to the racial hierarchies of Johann Friedrich Blumenbach (1752-1840). Blumenbach's racial design, modeled on the Great Chain of Being, placed the Caucasion at the pinnacle of human evolutionary development, with people of color occupying lower rungs in the paradigm. Coleridge was genuinely uncomfortable with, and ambivalent about, Blumenbach's thinking. Yet this discomfort failed to dissuade him from adapting this paradigm to the first chapter of Genesis. Finding the model a mechanically-efficient way of conveying Biblical anthropology, he converted Blumenbach's paradigm to his own use.

Specifically, Coleridge read Blumenbach's *De generis humani varietate nativa* (3rd edn. 1795), translated from the Latin to the German by Johann Gottfried Gruber (Leipzig, 1798) under the title, *Über die natürlichen Verschiedenheiten im Menschengeschlechte.*[7] Blumenbach maintained, in the first edition (1770), that the human race could be subdivided into four racial subcategories, a nomenclaturing he extended to five in the editions of 1781 and of 1795. Predicated on the notion of racial degeneration, he wrote in 1781 that, "The Caucasion must, on every physiological principle, be considered as the primary or intermediate of these five principle Races. The two extremes into which it has deviated, are on the one hand the Mongolian, on the other the Ethiopian. The other two Races [form] transitions between them; the American [Indian?] between the Caucasion and Mongolian; and the Malayan between the Caucasion and Ethiopian."

Coleridge had subscribed to Blumenbach's execrable design prior to converting it to more creative use. In the process of conversion, judging from this 1828 marginalium, he suppressed, but did not reject, the racist content:

Without rejecting [Blumenbach's] Pentad of Races but likewise without attributing more to it than the merit of being the most convenient Division hitherto proposed, I am [unwilling] to detach the subject from its historical Staple-ring, the Noachidae: and would therefore class the Haupt-varietäten, into the Generous, the Degenerous, and the Mixed. If the mythic Curse had not disfraternized the second or middle Brother [i.e., Ham], Mankind would have been, as one Species, so only one *Race*.

>   Prothesis
>   Noah
>   ———————
>
> Thesis   Indifference   Antithesis
> Shem   Ham   Japhet

The common Character of the Race, Historic. The Semitic or Positive Pole, the Religious-historic, Traditions secured and guarded by Rites, Institutions and Sacred Codes—. The Iapetic or Negative Pole, the literary, philosophic and sciential Historic:—The Hammonic, the Indifference of the Semitic and Iapetic: sciential, philosophic, and historical, but all in the form and service of Religion—. If therefore the Semitic be distinguished as the religious & the Iapetic as the Sciential, the Hammonic would be characterized as the Symbolic. And as the Degeneracy was gradual, such in fact *was* the character of the Land of Ham, or Ancient Egypt.—At present (and in all times since the commencement of Continued History) we find, First, the Generous or Semito-Iapetic Race—comprising the Jews, Syrians, Chaldeans, Arabians; the Persians, Greeks, and all the Gothic Nations, German, Swedish, Norwegian, Danish, English, and Scotch exclusive of the Highlanders ....
(*M*, 1:539-40)

The very idea of the racial "Degeneracy" of mankind is repugnant, and it is unfortunate that, for whatever reason, Coleridge indulged in this kind of thinking. In a *Table Talk* item, February 24, 1827, it is clear that he endorses Blumenbach's paradigm, listing in descending order Caucasion or European, Malay and American, and Negro and Mongolian-Asiatic.[8] How does one account for Coleridge's mixed opinion on the issue of race? J. H. Haeger explains the enigma of Coleridge's racial views. On the one hand, Coleridge supported the Abolitionist and Emancipationist movements wholeheartedly; but, on the other hand, like many Abolitionists of his times, he took for granted "the superiority of Western 'white' culture."[9] It is interesting to note that Blumenbach also expounded this mixed view. According to Stephen Jay Gould, despite Blumenbach's adherence to the idea of white supremacy, he remained a cultural relativist and a defender of equality, attributing racial differences to climate, and rejecting rankings "based on beauty or presumed mental ability."[10]

Displacing Blumenbach's racial designations with his own version of Genesis, chapters 10-11, Coleridge appropriates the latter's polarized model, the "Logical Pentad," to describe the dispersion of Noah's sons. Hence, Noah becomes the Prothesis; Shem and Japhet, thesis and antithesis, respectively; Ham, the mesothesis; and the ideal Christian, the envisioned synthesis. Trevor Levere correctly assesses Coleridge's indebtedness to Blumenbach's pseudoanthropology when he observes that the Logical Pentad provided him with a convenient way of explicating the mythic origins of Western civilization.[11] It also exemplifies his intellectual strategy of rebuilding the traditional model, internally, through the incorporation of contemporary theory.

As I mentioned, Coleridge's interest in Blumenbach's Pentad predates the recorded conversation (1827) and the marginalium (1828). He used this model in an 1818 Note (1818) and had probably been familiar with it as early as 1799 when attending Blumenbach's Göttingen lectures. In the 1818 Note he concedes that its application to Genesis is schematic, but he applies it, nonetheless, to early Western history, devising a fourfold dialectic of civilizations: the Hebrews as the original culture, the Greeks as "the Ideal Pole," the Romans "as the Real [Pole]," and Christianity as the "Synthesis" or axis of these dialectically-contiguous cultures (*CN* 3:4378).

In a draft to one of his literary lectures, Coleridge expands his creation theory, observing, here, how the "inspired Annals" were preoccupied with "the History of the posterity of Heber thro' Abraham, and with the other nations sprung either from Shem or Canaan, only as far as their history is interwoven with that of the Hebrew Tribes" [Genesis 10-11] (*LoL* 2:50). Concerned primarily with the Israelites from the period of Joshua to Samuel (Deut. 31.14; 1 Sam. 8-11), he speaks of them as "a race of men" who, both morally and intellectually, were the forefathers of the Western world. Philologists, political scientists, philosophers, and artists, this race, "as by divine impulse" or under the guidance of Providence, gradually "spread out and settled themselves, some northward, some southward, but all toward the west, and all within the temperate Zone" (2:51). He further describes the providentially-destined migrations of its "two main divisions," one westward, the other northwestward, tracing, altogether, a number of migratory lines and offshoots, all of which submerge in the heavily-edited draft, to resurface in Note 4384.

From the Ancient Hebrews, Coleridge turns to the Greeks, in Note 4378, initially describing them as prolific poets, artists, mathematicians, and logicians. Yet he qualifies their efforts: for "they acted upon the stores which the mind found within itself, awakened indeed by the excitement from external objects but not affirmed by them" (*CN* 3:4378). He seems to suggest that the limitations of the Greek mind stemmed from an inability to objectify the imagination fully, an achievement he called, in *Biographia Literaria*, "the fulness of the human intelligence" (1:286). This is clarified in his tenth *Literary Lecture*, in which he says that the formalism of Greek art was a deficiency: "The Greeks changed the ideas into finites, and these finites into *anthropomorphi*, or forms of men. Hence their religion, their poetry, nay, their very pictures, became statuesque. With them the form was the end" (*LR* 1:155). Worst of all, this kind of formalism shaped their theology, Greek sensuousness confounding "God with Nature"; therefore, they were incapable of "finding unity in the manifold and infinity in the individual"—a failure promoting pantheism, polytheism, and heroic deification (1:184-5). Judging art to be an index of culture, and dialectically defining its nature "as a middle quality between a thought and a thing ... the union and reconciliation of that which is nature with that which is exclusively human" (1:218-19), he argues that the Greeks submerged the transfiguring power of the imagination in nature, failing to affirm or to exalt human nature.

The materialistic limitations of Greek aesthetics, thought Coleridge, more adversely affected their science. In his "Preliminary Treatise on Method" (1818), he contends that the Greeks' limited artistic accomplishments vastly exceeded "the rude and imperfect manner in which [the Mind's own acts] were applied to the investigation of Physical Laws and phenomena." Thus their reputed inability to transform nature imaginatively paralleled their failure to develop the natural sciences. Committing what Herbert Butterfield has called the "anachronistic fallacy"—an author's injudicious evaluation of historical phenomena in the light of his or her contemporary world—Coleridge concludes that, "While Phidias, Appelles, Homer, Demosthenes, Thucydides, and Plato, had, each in his individual sphere, attained almost the summit of conceivable excellence, the Natural History and the Natural Philosophy of the whole World may be said to have lain dormant; especially if we compare them with the efforts which the Moderns made in these directions, in the very morning of their strength" (1:49).[12] Such a categorical oversimplification dramatizes the limits inherent in universal history: with its broad scope, superficialities, generalizations, and distortions are nearly unavoidable; in Coleridge's universal scheme, classical Greek culture is reduced to an integer in an ethnographic equation.

Coleridge does much the same thing with Roman history. Although adding nothing substantive to the stores of Greek thought, the Romans were important for having fixed Greek "Arts and Sciences" and for preparing "a soil properly cleared and fenced for their after-growth & ramification by War, Empire, and Law" (*CN* 3:4378). He reiterates this in the "Treatise on Method." Though the Romans confessed to being "mere imitators of the Greeks in everything relative to Science and Art," they still played a very significant role "in the Civil, Military, and Ecclesiastical History of Mankind" (*TM* 49-50). Roman artifice and civilization represented, for Coleridge, the context within which Greek ideas would evolve. In his first *Literary Lecture*, he explains that, "in consequence of the extension of the Roman Empire, some universal or common spirit became necessary for the conservation of the vast body [of Greco-Roman knowledge], and this common spirit was ... produced in Christianity" (*LR* 1:67).

Like most theological historians, Coleridge subordinates ancient Greece and Rome to Providence. As the third phase in the evolution of Western Christendom, Rome had a specifically pre-determined purpose. Although the Romans suppressed and persecuted the primitive Church, they were destined to be converted. Thanks to Constantine, paganism was reduced to "a Caput Mortuum" (*CN* 3:4378), and a greater synthesis would be realized: "the conquest of the Romans gave to the Goths the Christian religion as it was then existing in Italy" (*LR* 1:71; *LoL* 2:73-5). Each historical phase in Coleridge's scheme was foreordained for a single purpose: the establishment of Christianity.

By correlating the stages of Western civilization to stages in the maturation of the individual, Coleridge demonstrates his affinity to Christian writers from Augustine to Bossuet, as well as his indebtedness to the *Universalgeschichten*. From the Germans, he enlisted analogies and metaphors to unify his world history conceptually. One of these, originally a classical analogy which the Germans revived, compares the development of a race or civilization to an individual's growth stages. To Coleridge, this was another useful device for conveying the organic unity of history. Surveying classical history, he recounts that, "[We] have ... accompanied the Race ... first through its boyhood [the Hebraic], then thro' its Youth [the Greco-Roman], and lastly in preparation of making the practical use of its acquirements [Gothic to early Modern European]" (*CN* 3:4378). The "modern" era, spanning more than a millennium (c. 500 A.D. to 1818), is described as a period of "Travel and Excursion, or what is called the Grand Tour." For the Westerner, these would be "Travels almost guideless into the world within us, and into the external World—a Great

Revolution had taken place" (*CN* 3:4378). From his post-revolutionary vantage point, Coleridge is referring to a spiritual revolution, the interior illumination of the individual, inspiring large-scale social change. His progressive vision for a humane society depending, foremost, on Christian enlightenment, he re-considers this topic in the 1818 *Friend*, comparing the progress of ancient civilization and theology to individual growth stages. Hence, this evolution moves from primitive monotheism (Jewish Childhood), through intermediate stages of civilization and of culture (Greco-Roman Youth), to a stage in which Christianity would consolidate and flourish. His ultimate purpose is to "review the Method in which Providence has brought the more favored portion of mankind to the present state of Arts and Sciences" (1:500).

His survey of the evolution of Western culture begins with the Jewish people. The Hebrews were educated in "the moral sense," Divine Providence appealing to the conscience in order to cultivate in the Hebrew theocrats what was "truly human in human nature." Through this process of enlightenment and humanization, they recognized their Creator "as a spirit" Who could not be realized "under any *image*" but Who deserved their veneration nonetheless (*F* 1:500-01).

Contrary to these faithful theocrats were apostates who chose a materialistic path, becoming "rapidly civilized" and, by implication, despiritualized. These apostates built "cities, invented musical instruments, were artificers in brass and iron, and refined on the means of sensual gratification, and the conveniences of the AGREEABLE, which fraternized readily with cruelty and rapacity: these being, indeed but alternate moods of the same sensual selfishness" (1:501-02). Because they had no conception of God's unity, and because of their sensuousness, they rapidly degenerated into polytheism (1:502-03), a descent he traces in "Treatise on Method": the apostates, "determined to receive nothing as true, but what they derived, or believed themselves to derive, from their senses, or ... what they could prove *a posteriori* ... became Idolaters of the Heavens, and of the material elements; and finally, out of the Idols of the Mind, they formed material Idols: and bowed down to stocks and stones, as to the unformed incorporeal Divinity" (*TM* 48).

Of the Greeks, Coleridge had much more to say. Once their role had been fulfilled as "the representative of the youth and approaching manhood of the intellect," ancient Greece suffered a millennium of decline: "from Orpheus, Linus, Musaeus ... to the time when the republics lost their independence, and the learned men sunk into copyists and commentators of the works of their forefathers"—that is, from pre-1000 B.C. to 146 B.C. (*F* 1:503). The influence of Hebrew monotheism on

Greek poetry and mythology, however, arrested this decline, preventing Greek polytheism "from producing all its barbarizing effects" (1:504). To this tempering influence, he attributes the development of the classical genres: "the mysteries and the mythical Hymns and Paeans shaped themselves gradually into epic Poetry and History, on the one hand, and into ethical Tragedy and Philosophy on the other" (1:504). But, beyond a pre-determined limit, Greek philosophy and art were not destined to pass. At that point, the mission "for which [they] existed had been completed," for they represented, to Coleridge, "a portion only of the education of man"—a specifically prescribed stage in "the education of the mind of the race" (1:504).

3. Note 4384; *Literary Lectures*, 1-2; Egerton Ms. (1819); the eighth *Philosophical Lecture*

Professor Kathleen Coburn has suggested that Notes 4378 and 4384, treating medieval culture and poetry, were drafts for *Literary Lectures* 1-2 (Jan.-Feb. 1818), and that Coleridge appears to have consulted Friedrich von Schlegel's *Geschichte der alten und neuen Litteratur* ... (1815), paying particular attention to the latter's interpretation of, and apology for, Gothic and medieval culture, respectively. Aside from this indebtedness, she notes that Coleridge should be credited for a number of important additions, all of which have a direct bearing on his idea of history: a long cultural-racial introduction; the Biblical foundation to cultural history; the emphasis on the Greco-Roman/Gothic contrast; the rhapsody on the "unifying Gothic temper of mind"; and the development of the Greek/German and public/private contrasts (*CN* 3:4384n.). By developing three significant ideas—what Coleridge understood as being the Jewish phase of Western history, the notion of migratory lines ramifying from the Middle East, and the view of the gradual consolidation of European Christendom after the fall of Rome—he advances, in Note 4384, beyond both Note 4378 and the 1818 *Friend*.

Coleridge cites "the commencement of profane History" as coinciding with "the time of the Judges in the Sacred Writings" (i.e., c. 1200 B.C.), then elaborates on the story of Noah's progeny as the forefathers of the human race, relying on the accounts given in Genesis, 10:1-31 and 11:10-32. Of the three sons—Japheth, Ham, and Sem—Coleridge attends to the first, relating that his descendents, the "Japetidae," had "diverged from their native Asia [Minor]," splitting into two branches, one of which "took possession of Greece, the Greek Isles, and colonized the coasts of the Lesser Asia Minor": "thus by a literal fulfillment of the Noetic tradition, [they] dwelt in the Tents of Shem" (*CN* 3:4384).

Coleridge's Biblical accretion to this Note suggests that he was trying to reaffirm the importance of Genesis as an authentic historical source; however, he remained somewhat ambiguous about the Noachian theory and, generally, about any literal approach to Scripture. We do know that, although he had difficulty with the idea of inerrancy, he still exhibited a "profound respect for the literal sense of the Bible," a respect, observes J. Robert Barth, reflected by his interest in historical and geographical background, and in literary symbols, language, and myth.[13] Nonetheless, it is difficult to account, precisely, for his ambivalence about the historical authority of Genesis. On the one hand, he professed an orthodox attitude towards the Bible, one that is well documented. With respect to Creation, as Coburn has shown (*CN* 3:4384n.), Note 4418 (August 1818) represents his "first systematic exegesis of the first chapter of the Bible ... in relation to philosophical and scientific theories of the creation of the world." Levere describes the strong, but qualified, influence of the *Naturphilosophen* on his cosmogony: the notebooks, marginalia, and letters indicate that he was indebted to, but did not entirely accept, the cosmogonies of Böhme, Eichhorn, Schelling, and Steffens. Theologically, his Creation account had to be consistent with, and predicated upon, both the book of Genesis and Trinitarian doctrine; hence, he rejected their speculations, even though, in Note 4418, his explication of the first chapter of Genesis is an erudite alloy of polar dialecticism, of the Gospel of St. John, and of Hermetic and Paracelsian ideas found in the works of Böhme.[14]

Hoping to conflate the Bible and modern science, Coleridge devised an orthodox cosmogony with God as "the absolute Beginner of all things" (*CN* 3:4418). Following Steffens and Eschenmayer, he re-cast chapters three and five of Genesis metascientifically; thus, from an initial act of polarization, Light and Darkness issued out of Chaos. As an accommodationist, he also found the cosmological speculations of Böhme especially attractive, paraphrasing in an 1819 marginalium the latter's magnetic rendition of the Big Bang: "As soon as the Darkness Separated into Light and Gravity, each bipolar, the four elementary products of the four polar Energies became at the same instant Water under the predominance of Light, and Metal under the predominance of Gravity" (*M* 1:663).

The metascientific analogies do not becloud Coleridge's efforts to bring diverse ideas together consistently. Unquestionably, Genesis 1:1-5 is the primary source of his efficient cosmogony which draws on ideas as multifarious as dynamic logic, Trinitarianism, Schelling's nature philosophy, and Steffen's compass of powers. Levere indicates that Coleridge pursued his cosmic vision further in volume one of the "Opus Maximum" manuscripts, conceiving of material creation as emanating from the Light-Darkness polarity.[15] Encouraged by these balanced correlations, he used polarity logic to interpret verses six through thirteen concerning the development of life, from plants to mankind. Supporting his orthodox cosmogony with old and new ideas, and despite inconsistencies, Coleridge's approach was consistently eclectic and orthodox.

Another instance of Coleridge's desire to reconcile the Bible to modern science involves evolution, a topic having important historical ramifications. In a manuscript entry associated with the "Opus Maximum," he unequivocally declares that, "The History I find in my Bible is in perfect coincidence with the opinions which I form on the Grounds of Experience and Common Sense."[16] And, in a well-known letter to Wordsworth (May 30, 1815), Coleridge refutes natural philosophers, like Tyson and Oken, who believed that mankind had "progressed from an Ouran Outang state—so contrary to all History, to all Religion, nay, to all Possibility." He affirms "a Fall in some sense as a fact, the possibility of which cannot be understood from the nature of the Will, but the reality of which is attested by Experience & Conscience" (*CL* 4:574).

Although Coleridge understood evolution to be a natural process, his interpretation was theologically orientated: though part of nature, humanity was distinguished from the animal kingdom by virtue of its kinship to God. Thus, in his "Formation of a More Comprehensive Theory of Life" (1816) and elsewhere, he contended that natural phenomena ascended to a greater complexity, simultaneously a movement towards individuation and to unity.[17] In his view, this platonized biology, the heritage and hallmark of *Naturphilosophie*, neither contradicted the idea of a special creation (the notion that mankind was the self-conscious epitome of nature), nor precluded organic development.

Yet Coleridge, alert to the danger of extremism, tried to maintain a middle ground between the pantheistic leanings of the Germans, on the one hand, and Biblical literalism, on the other. No doubt this effort to balance his religious and scientific inclinations was difficult and not always successful. With respect to evolutionary theory, Professor Coburn's conclusion appears to me quite reasonable: "Wherever the truth lies in Coleridge's conflicting statements about evolution, there is no doubt that man was for him the apex of natural processes of the phenomenal world."[18]

Note 4384 is significant for its Noachian passage and for the elaboration of the European migratory lines emerging from the Javan trunk: these "are best known by the name of Goths, or of the Gothic Nations, the Getae and the Massegetae of the classics," those who had "pressed onward North-west, thro' Northern Germany & thro' Holstein into Denmark and Sweden." Coleridge characterizes these Teutonic-Nordic people, collectively, as "Goths." A tertiary branch migrating between the "two mighty Brotherhoods of the Graeco-Roman and the Gothic-Teutonic," the "Celtic Tribes" derived from an intermixture of the descendents of such "mixed marriages," appearing "to have spread out due East and due West, and in the latter direction peopled the vast interspace that ... for a series of ages divided and estranged the Goths, and the Romans from each other." He also identifies a quaternary branch "that sprung from the union of the posterity of Ham and Canaan with the descendents of Shem"—that is, "the Egyptians and Phoenicians"—while the "least mixed descendents of Ham passed Southward into Africa" (3:4384).

With the main migratory lines delineated, Coleridge expounds upon later historical developments, especially upon Teutonic and Roman hegemony against the Celts. Eventually, the Goths would contribute to the fall of a corrupt Rome. He relates, in the second *Literary Lecture*, that: "The hardy habits, the steady perseverance, the better faith of the enduring Goth rendered him too formidable an enemy for the corrupt Rome, who was more inclined to purchase the subjection of his enemy, than to go through the suffering necessary to secure it. The conquest of the Romans gave to the Goths the Christian religion" (*LR* 1:70-1). Thus the "Roman Province" gradually gave way to Gothic kingdoms, the "Western Empire," to "modern Christendom." From the period of Theodoric and the fall of Rome, "a *process*" of reunification had commenced, an era that would constitute "the History of the Philosophy of the Dark or Middle Ages" (*CN* 3:4384). At this juncture, he contends, a cultural synthesis had been realized—"a marvellous compound, in which the philosophy and the loveliness of Grecian Genius, the legislatorial and ordonnant Mind of civilizing Rome joined with the ... deep feelings, the high imagination, the chivalrous Courtesies, and ... strong breathings after immortality of the Goths had produced the Base, and Christianity the all-combining, all-penetrating ... all-transforming spirit of union and ennoblement." For Coleridge, the "History of any country begins with the Gothic," the history of England, with the "Anglo-Saxons" (3:4384).

Doubtless, Note 4384 is integral to the development of Coleridge's history of Western civilization. In it, he details the Jewish period of the race; chronologically exceeds the sketches in Note 4378 and the 1818 *Friend*; attempts to account, however problematically, for Asian and African migrations; and delineates the European migrations and the eventual synthesis in Christendom. He adds considerable detail to his depiction of early modern history in *Literary Lectures*, one and two, and in a manuscript note of 1819. Thus far, the evidence indicates Coleridge's greater affinity, not to St. Augustine, but to Orosius. Stressing the idea that Providence pervades historical cultures, both Orosius and Coleridge envisage the City of God as an evolving reality, the configuration of which might be discerned historically.

Coleridge's temporal perspective in the 1819 Egerton Ms. Note is determined entirely by Scripture: "both before and after the flood the vicious of mankind receded from all cultivation, as they hurried toward civilization"—a goal connoting materialism, polytheism, imperialism, and licentiousness. Specifically, he defines a barbaric State as one lacking "the means of National and Individual Progression," means otherwise attained through "Letters, Books, Printing, Men of Learning, Men of Science, Artists." But education alone was not enough to guarantee "cultivation." Beyond the establishment of "Schools for the different Ranks of Society," a number of social measures had to be enacted: "opportunities of *moral* education and *religious* instruction for all in all ranks"; "the equality of Women to men in social and domestic Life"; and "the unconditional sovereignty of Law over individual Will" (*IS* 314). In the aggregate, these elements comprised a "civilized *and* cultivated" State, one that was "organized by mutual interdependence into a System of Society" (314-15). Under the sovereignty of the Law, a fully-cultivated State, Coleridge claims, could guarantee "a sphere for the exercise of Free-agency, into which no other Individual is permitted to intrude[;] in all points [this sphere is] necessary to his Well-being and Progressive Improvement as a responsible Creature destined for a State after Death" (315). Once again, Coleridge maintains that a unified "System of Society," a truly civilized culture, could only be achieved through Christian education and through faith.

One can apply the definitions and distinctions of the Egerton Ms. Note to Coleridge's understanding of Greco-Roman history. Although intellectually productive, the Greeks were only partially cultivated. Greek materialism retarded social development, contributing to polytheism, to anthropomorphic idolatry, to the repression of women, to licentiousness, and to the protracted warfare of the City-States. Each of these fragmented and immoral conditions reflected an underlying ethical pathology, one that prevented the human spirit from developing to its fullest potential. Roman civilization—preoccupied with war, empire, and law—although an even more stagnant phase in the development of Western culture, was paradoxically destined to be the cradle of incipient Christianity and, hence, of the culturing impulse. For Coleridge, Gothic culture was, therefore, the first fully-recognizable Christian State, and the seed of Western culture and of the democratic idea. Coleridge's City of God, in its initial manifestation, is identified with the "generic character of the Northern [i.e., Gothic] nations" and defined by salient features differentiating it from Greece and Rome: "their respect for women" and their laying "the foundation of the representative form of government, the only rational mode of preserving individual liberty in opposition to the licentious democracy of the ancient republics" (*LR* 1:68).

The most incisive document in this series is the eighth *Philosophical Lecture* (Feb. 15, 1819). Coleridge prefaces this lecture on the commencement of "MODERN PHILOSOPHY" with the idea that history is consonant with the revelation of Divine Providence, the final cause of which is "to prepare the way to religion" (247). The history of philosophy as the gradual revelation of the Absolute Will records attempts "to seek after the origin of things and the fundamental laws of the world by the efforts of the reason and understanding alone" (247). Relying on the traditional story of human origins, he recapitulates the doctrine of the Noachian dispersion up to the time of Theodoric, at which time Greek genius, Roman ordonnance, and Gothic fervor were synthesized in Christianity, a triumph he ascribes to "THE ALL-COMBINING, ALL-PENETRATING, ALL-TRANSFORMING SPIRIT OF UNION AND ENNOBLEMENT" (257).

Coleridge's account of the ancient and classical past reflects his commitment to theological history. This is supported by the fact that his chronology of forty-five centuries, from the Hebrews to the Goths and Anglo-Saxons, is rooted in the book of Genesis. Employing the kind of periodical scheme popular to scholastic and medieval historiography and revived by the German idealists, Coleridge sees history as a continuum that, in its pre-modern dimension, consists of four dialectically-related cultures—the Hebrew, the Greek, the Roman, and the Gothic—a scheme he would extend to include the Anglo-Saxon imperium. Most important is that the entire system, from its inception, is a redemptive process, unfolding providentially and revealed through Scripture.

This traditionalism did not preclude experimentation. With the purpose of revitalizing the inflexible format, Coleridge assimilated modern concepts into the patristic framework: Blumenbach's Logical Pentad, sanitized of racism, is used to describe the dynamics of providential history; to conciliate science and Scripture, cosmological and biological metaphors used by the *Naturphilosophen* are incorporated (often tentatively) into the patristic design; and the development of culture is described, analogically, in terms of the growth stages of the individual person.

Despite Coleridge's imaginatively-syncretic approach to universal history, one would not consult him for an accurate, carefully-documented history of the Greeks, of the Romans, or of the Goths. Obviously, limitations inherent in this genre rendered his historiography schematic, inexact, and doctrinaire. Indeed, his reduction of cultures to ideas, and of these ideas to a preconceived theodicy, leaves little or no room for original thinking about natural or human history. From his perspective at the turn of the century, however, Coleridge's theology of history can still be considered a daring reassertion of traditional ideas, an act of faith and of intelligence before the de-sacralizing spirit of his age.

The second contiguous phase of Coleridge's tripartite theodicy comprises thirteen centuries (c. 500 to 1800) and five conventionally-periodized epochs: the medieval, the Renaissance, and the seventeenth, eighteenth, and nineteenth centuries. To describe the inner workings of Providence, this time in the modern age, Coleridge once again employs polarity logic.

CHAPTER EIGHT

"The Lessons of Wisdom and Caution": European History, Medieval to Modern

The progression of documents comprising Coleridge's modern history (c. 500 A.D. to 1833) demonstrates interdisciplinary erudition and is an important example of historical periodization that should be ranked with Fichte's *Characteristics of the Present Age* (1806) and Hegel's *Philosophy of History* (1822-1823).[1] He proposed that Western history contained a dialectically-syncretic process, "The Moral Law of Polarity," governed by Divine Providence and characterized, in each epoch, by an ascendant philosophy or "spirit of the age" which informed civilization and culture. Spanning six millennia (assuming tacit subscription to the Ussherite Creation date), his periodical design was subdivided into three parts: an ancient and classical segment (4004 B.C. [?] to 500 A.D.), a medieval to modern segment (c. 500 to 1800), and a prospective segment implicitly identified with the Anglo-Saxon imperium. In addition, his reconstruction of modern history eruditely combines the three aspects of periodical historiography: chronological arrangement, dialectical development, and the individuality of respective milieu.[2]

Surprising, in view of his orthodoxy, is the fact that Coleridge avoided the temptation of looking for God's direct intervention in modern events. Unlike the patristic writers who expected the imminent consummation of historical time, and mindful of the most recent example of revolutionary millenarianism, he searched the recent past for coherent and demonstrable patterns relegating, rather than exiling, Divine Providence to the background of human affairs.

Despite this reorientation, it is important to remember that, for Coleridge, history remained the matrix of divine revelation. Though he did not fully integrate contemporaneous speculations on typology and Providence directly into his philosophy of modern history, this evidences neither a crisis of faith nor an abandonment of purpose; rather, it represents an aspect of his accommodative thinking. Like his contemporaries who modified or who entirely abandoned the theological framework, he realized that complex modern events and conditions, to be comprehended syncretically, required the application of contemporary, not of anachronistic, methods. For this reason, with regard to modern history, he maintained his theological convictions and, in the light of what his conscience would allow, approached the past with modern theory.

1. 1808

The first document in the series, "A Brief History of the Last 130 Years" (i.e., c. 1680 to 1808), comprises four historical periods: the English Revolution (c. 1648-1688); the American Revolution (1775-1783); the French Revolution (1789-1799); and the Napoleonic period (1798-1808). It originally appeared in an 1808 manuscript and was published in the 1818 *Friend*. Coleridge's historical commentary is so far-reaching and cryptic that it is necessary, at each junction, to include background information. I will begin with the English Revolution, interspersing historical information where needed.

After "*The English Revolution of* 1688," writes Coleridge, Hobbes' theory of atomic philosophy was transported to England, profoundly affecting neoclassical thought. The "Mechanic Philosophy" was eventually "espoused as a common cause, by the partizans of the revolution of the state" (*F* 1:447), becoming the philosophy reputedly underlying natural-rights doctrine. Thus atomism undermined British culture to the point where Idealism collapsed completely, along with the platonic idea of an organically-developing culture. To natural-rights doctrine, he opposes "the true historical feeling," a conservative and Burkean formula linking "generation to generation by ancestral reputation, by tradition, [and] by heraldry" (1:447).

In the second revolutionary phase of the dialectic, French "Anglo-mania" precipitated the American Revolution, 1775-1783. Because they believed the American Constitution to be a "universal model" for democratic revolution, and not the anomaly Coleridge claimed it to be, the Enlightened French committed a sociopolitical heresy. Objecting vehemently to the anti-monarchic, American document—"a treaty, imposed by the people on their own government as on a conquered enemy"—he therefore condemns French democrats and radicals, in the third period (1789-1794), for "giving sanction to falsehood, and universality to anomaly!!!" (1:447); and he derides the kind of impractical idealism and decentralized social thinking reputedly responsible for the Revolution's failure. Destroyed by social unrest and, more so, by a presumptuous contempt for history, France, says Coleridge, is a self-immolating nation.

To France's self-destructive tendencies, Coleridge contrasts the English tradition of Church and State interdependency. In this fourth period, 1799 to 1808, he postulates that, "religion ... is and ever has been the moral centre of gravity in Christendom, to which all things must and will accommodate themselves" (1:447). Despite its brevity, this statement reflects not only the Orosian heritage—expressed, variously, by Richard Hooker (1552-1600), by Bishop William Warburton (1698-1779), and by others—but also Coleridge's unequivocal identification of teleological history with the life of the Christian Church and, more specifically, with the Christian Church in England. He elaborates on this national dimension, asserting that a "learned class," forerunner of the clerisy, was essential to the life of a Christian State, a conservative bulwark against adversarial, ahistorical theories (1:447).

Additional background in the history of ideas will help us to unravel the scientific, philosophical, and political theory to which Coleridge subscribes and which he sometimes misconstrues.[3] The seventeenth-century world-view comprised two parallel lines of thinking that were to merge in Newton's *Principia* (1687). The first, which was empirical, atomistic, and materialistic, can be traced to Pierre Gassendi (1592-1655) and to a revival of interest in the "scientific" philosophy of Democritus and Epicurus, especially as outlined in Lucretius' *De Rerum Natura*. Coleridge rejected the atomistic theorem that the universe could be understood as consisting of indivisibly-mobile particles. The second, which was rationalistic, mathematical, and sometimes idealistic rather than materialistic, and which evolved from Pythagorean mathematics through Plato and the Neoplatonists, postulated a rationally-ordered cosmos. To the atomists, the universe was empirical, provisional, undetermined, and without either Design or Designer, whereas, to the rationalists—such as Descartes (1596-1650), Boyle (1627-1691), Newton (1642-1727), and Leibnitz (1646-1716)—the universe was a clock-work design, an holistically-ordered system, each component of which, mankind included, was a cog in the machine.

When Coleridge alludes to Hobbes's bringing of the atomic philosophy to England, and igniting a complex philosophical and social reaction, he is referring, specifically, to the Newcastle Circle, founded, in the 1640s, by British emigrants like William Cavendish (1592-1676). Refuting Descartes' vorticist and plenist ideas set forth in his *Principles of Philosophy* (1644), the atomists described the nature of matter, metaphorically, with inventive phrases such "*vis motrix,*" "*minima divisibilia,*" or "all-pervading aether."[4]

After the execution of Charles I, in 1649, and with the decline of the Royalists, the Newcastle emigrants returned to England where their influence spread. I am uncertain as to whether Coleridge knew the historical details, but he certainly was aware of the fact that the major challenge to the viability of atomism was the charge of atheism. Joining the theologians were the professional scientists who engaged in a heated debate about the "hypothetical physics." Many scientists of the day, particularly the members of the Royal Society of London, were rationalists. Isaac Barrow (1630-1677), Christopher Wrenn (1632-1723), and Sir Isaac Newton rejected the atomists' presupposition that matter was basically particulate; they subscribed, instead, to a Baconian approach pursuing experimental certitude in the physical sciences. The Baconian method and the adoption of an Archimedean or mathematical approach to the study of matter would set the foundation of modern physics.

In the 1808 Scale (rpt. 1818), Coleridge was only tangentially concerned with the struggles of the rationalists. His primary interest was to explore the relationship, if any, between the entrenched Newcastle Circle and anti-monarchic politics, a correlation that, at first glance, might appear strained. Coleridge's thesis is twofold: the underlying philosophy of an age created political structures in its own image; and, reciprocally, these political and social institutions provided contexts that nurtured and perpetuated the informing "spirit of the age." According to the scheme he would work out in 1833, the overthrow of the prevailing philosophical and political dynasty could be anticipated, with almost cyclical regularity, according to "The Moral Law of Polarity" (*TT* 149-50). Thus he concludes that the Civil War and the Restoration were the socio-political contexts of atomistic materialism—of a fragmented and Godless cosmology—which either engendered, or made conditions conducive to, natural rights or Social Contract Theory and to associationism, a psychological equivalent to corpuscular physics.

A closer look at Coleridge's thesis reveals much about his strengths and weaknesses as an historian of ideas. His premise in the 1808 Scale—atomism germinated natural-rights idealism—derives from his readings (or misreadings) of John Locke (1632-1704), in whose works, he thought, these adversarial philosophies converged.[5] Herbert Butterfield corroborates Coleridge's notion of Locke's importance when he states that the latter stands at "the pivotal point" of "a colossal secularization of thought in every possible realm of ideas at the time."[6] Locke, it seems, arrived at this pivotal point after Shaftesbury (1621-1683) fell from power. Pressured politically, Locke first emigrated to France: there, from 1673 to 1679, he was influenced by French atomists. He emigrated once more, this time to Holland, staying from 1683 to 1689, where he completed his *Essay Concerning Human Understanding* (1690) (published in its final form with the accession of William of Orange), as well as his *Two Treatises of Government*; the latter work was erroneously thought to have been published in 1690 and to have justified the 1689 Revolution.[7]

Although Locke did indeed expound sensationalist psychology in *Human Understanding*, and although correctly identified by Coleridge as a pivotal figure, Coleridge incorrectly concludes that sensationalism *and* Social Contract Theory were genetic descendents of, rather than analogues to, corpuscular or atomic theory. Since both Social Contract Theory and corpuscular physics emerged at the time of the English Civil War, Coleridge mistook their relationship to be causative, not merely coextensive. Fortunately, the distinction Coleridge blurred is, for us, self-evident: the social theorists of the times were concerned about the origins, the legitimacy, and the authority of government, not, as was the case with the atomists, with the composition of matter.[8] Social Contractualists believed that society was a human contrivance, not a divine or natural construct. Shifting the authority of government from God and king to the average citizen, they formulated the idea of a consensual contract. Taking its most radical form in the notion of popular sovereignty, and sternly opposed by Hobbes, Spinoza, and Filmer, natural-rights thinkers challenged the authority of aristocratic government. It is this position that provoked Coleridge's rancor.

Coleridge's antipathy both for Locke's epistemology and political philosophy is, therefore, easily understood. The epistemology challenged innate ideas and the notion that human consciousness is ontologically grounded in God, while the political philosophy subverted the inherited authority of the king. Both views were inimical to Coleridge's theological and political views.

But what accounts for Coleridge's metaphoric leap from scientific philosophy to politics? The error of amalgamating science, psychology, and political theory might have been inherited, in part, from Locke himself. On the one hand, Locke had posited an epistemology refuting the possibility of innate ideas. On the other hand, he had devised a political theory based on the very idea that a person was born with innate rights upon which civil rights and social equity might be based. How, in other words, could Locke argue, simultaneously, that an individual was born a *tabula rasa* yet endowed with innate rights?[9] This contradiction might have encouraged Coleridge to blame French Jacobinism (a political manifestation of social contractualism at its worst), *not* on Locke's social idealism, but on his sensationalist psychology instead. A useful example of how Coleridge mixed atomism and natural-rights idealism occurs in *Aids to Reflection*; he writes about "the utter emptiness and unmeaningness of the vaunted Mechanico-corpuscular philosophy, with its twins, Materialism ... and Idealism, rightlier named subjective Idolism," and of how one obtrudes on us "a world of spectres and apparitions; the other a mazy dream" (333). Blaming the social and political discontents of his times not on a social doctrine (natural rights), but on a scientific philosophy (atomism), he protests against Jacobinism, his assessment of the fourth period, 1795-1818, becoming an apology for conservatism and a call for the recultivation of Anglican tradition.

Its lack of development and confusion of categories notwithstanding, this Scale contains a number of intelligent insights: successive milieux are dialectically interrelated, each having a point of revolutionary crisis; ideas evolve and do not appear *in vacuo*; and the State cannot be created *ab novo* through the annihilation of the past.

2. 1816

Throughout *The Statesman's Manual* (1816), Appendix E, Coleridge elucidates his idea of history, expanding his scope from the ninth to the nineteenth century and alluding to a broad range of philosophical movements. To illustrate the allegation that European philosophy was currently in decline, he surveys five contiguous milieux: the revival of Neoplatonic thought in fifteenth-century Florence (in Poliziano, the de Medicis, Ficino, and della Mirandola) and in Elizabethan England (Spenser, the Sidneys, Milton, Harrington, and Nevil); and he contrasts these awakenings to the revival of trade and of the commercial spirit during the English Civil War and the Restoration. During the Enlightenment, he says, this emphasis on mercantilism reached its epitome. In this, the third contiguous period of his modern history, Coleridge berates the sensationalists, Social Contractors, radicals of every ilk, and utilitarians, all of whom reputedly idolized abstract reason at the expense of the imagination.

The pervading theme of Appendix E is how the notion of the "Idea" had devolved from a supernal to a materialistic meaning. To emphasize his distaste for the metaphysical trends of the previous century, he contrasts these schools of thought to the work of the Schoolmen and, particularly, to Erigena (800-877), to Lombard (1100-1160), and to Duns Scotus (1265-1308), the principal cultivators of Neoplatonic thought in early medieval Europe (*LS* 100-03). With respect to the debate on the Ancients and the Moderns, Coleridge is clearly on the side of the Ancients: Neoplatonic Christianity, in his estimation, is the hope of modern culture because it provides a way of unifying history transcendentally.

Coleridge's Neoplatonism allowed him to perceive a causative relationship between philosophy and religion: "all History seems to favor the persuasion, I entertain, that in every age the speculative Philosophy in general acceptance, the metaphysical opinions that happen to be predominant, will influence the *Theology* of that age" (*LS* 103). In the 1808 Scale, he had called the Glorious Revolution and the Mechanic Philosophy "kindred revolutions" in politics and philosophy, respectively. In addition, he suggested that the rise and fall of metaphysical systems, on the one hand, and of political institutions, on the other, were related to one another phenomenally. In 1816, he clarifies this, stating that history "*seems to favor*" the belief that "speculative Philosophy ... *will influence* the *Theology* of that age [verb underscorings mine]." Two cogent points are worth making. First, in Copy G, Coleridge expanded the meaning of "Theology" to include the Fine Arts and the science of culture generally, an extrapolation that would have important bearing on later discussion; this broadened definition is consistent with his understanding of "history" as an aspect of theology. Second, the neutral transitive verb "influence" (rather than a more active verb like "determines"), along with the subjunctive mood, suggests that Coleridge was unsure about precisely how ideas affect culture.

Referring to the atheistic trends of the modern age, and using the deft appositives "Conservators of the national Faith" and "accredited representatives of Learning," Coleridge calls upon the Established clergy to judge the comparative value of the "old" or Neoplatonic, and of the "new" or sensationalist, philosophy (*LS* 106-07). With respect to their "contempt for all prior systems," he polemicizes, extensively, against modern educational theorists, urging the Established clergy to initiate a *risorgimento* in Anglican thought, a revival of principles authorized and expounded by Hooker, by Whitaker (1548-1595), by Field (1561-1616), and by Selden (1584-1654); such a revival he deemed the only viable way of countering the hegemony of natural rights and of atheistic thinking. On "the authority of the greatest and noblest intellects for at least two thousand years," Coleridge concludes that modern Anglican Divines could not hope to preserve the Established Church and the social order if they neglected or abjured Plato, Aristotle, and "the study of the theological Metaphysicians & Systematic Divines of the 12th, 13th, and 14th Centuries" (*LS* 111n., 112).

Despite its organizational weaknesses and ideological hard-line, the 1816 Scale supersedes its 1808 precursor. The 1816 Scale provides more detail and explanation; widens the chronological scope; clarifies the author's ideological position; and suggests some interesting deductions about the philosophy of history (that is, the prevailing philosophy *might influence* culture and civilization). Probably the most idiosyncratic and erudite example of historical periodization is the well-known Letter to Liverpool, July 28, 1817.

3. The "Rescue" Letter

Liverpool perplexingly endorsed Coleridge's letter: "From Mr. Coleridge, stating that the object of his writings has been to rescue speculative philosophy from false principles of reasoning . . . at least I believe this is Mr. Coleridge's meaning, but I cannot well understand him" (*CL* 4:757n.). Liverpool's bewilderment is humorous and points to Coleridge's bad habit of forgetting his audience. The problem with "Coleridge's meaning" is not a new one: the Letter assumes that the reader is sufficiently well-versed in the history of philosophy to understand the multiplicity of references. For me, tracking down the references and searching for a coherent pattern proved a major, but ultimately enlightening, job. What emerges is a periodical design that, once annotated, is a virtual gloss on the history of ideas. Of the five traditions integrated in this document, three are sharply criticized. Interspersed are indictments of atomism, of didactic art, of Deism, and of Social Contract Theory, each of which is respectively countered by politically-conservative, orthodoxly-Christian, and Neoplatonic rejoinders. I will treat the content of the Letter in some detail and reflect on Coleridge's rhetorical and organizational practices as well.

At the outset, Coleridge ironically describes his "incurable heresy": the "meretricious philosophy" held sacred in the seventeenth and eighteenth centuries (4:758). Alluding to atomism and the Newcastle Circle—to how this philosophy took root in England with the Restoration of Charles II—he refers to Shaftesbury (1621-1683) whom he calls a "Factious Patron," a pejorative phrase referring to the latter's opposition to autocracy, support of Locke, founding of the Whigs, and strengthening of Nonconformity. Coleridge then alludes, cryptically, to Locke's crucial emigrations and to their effects: "The Magdalen eloped to the Anti-Christians on the continent, the Pallas . . . of the encylopedists [sic.], and the Jacobins' Goddess of Reason" (4:758). I read this as follows: with "Magdalen" (the penitent prostitute) standing for sensationalist psychology and "Pallas" (Pallas Athena, that is, who sprang from the head of Zeus) for French atomism, Coleridge attempts to connect Locke's

French emigration (1683-1689) to the works of the French Encyclopedists—Diderot, D'Alembert, Rousseau, Montesquieu, Turgot, and Voltaire—who, in the first volume of their *Encyclopédie* (1751), championed skepticism and scientific rationalism. Though Locke's death, in 1704, tends to obfuscate the connection between his work and that of the *philosophes*, contemporary scholars have established a direct linkage, thus corroborating Coleridge's hypothesis. Norman L. Torrey, for instance, observes that the "theory of sensationalism, stripped of its scholastic overtones, was passed on to the *philosophes* through John Locke and Condillac and became one of the burning issues of the struggle for freedom of thought."[10] Frederick A. Artz reiterates the notion that the later materialism of Diderot, La Mettrie, d'Holbach, and others was derived directly from English precursors such as Locke and Newton.[11]

Once again disregarding his audience, Coleridge, in the second paragraph, experiments with apophastic irony, a form of understatement in which an assertion is made though it is seemingly suppressed or denied.[12] Irony directs his indictment of corpuscular philosophy:

> I am fully aware, my Lord, that scarcely one in ten thousand is sufficiently interested in the first problems of speculative science to give himself any concern about the truth or falsehood of the solutions, or even to understand the terms in which they are enunciated. What matter is it to the World, it will be said,—of what consequence can it be to society at *large*, that the Physiology alone taught or tolerated at the present day sets out with a pure fiction, an ultimate particle to wit? that it proceeds with a blank miracle, i.e. the causeless & therefore praeternatural Hardness or infrangibility of these corpuscles, with an Apotheosis of death, by virtue of which the insensate moats are elevated into Demiurgic atoms, indivisible & yet space-comprehending minims, that are at once the stuff, the tools, & the workmen of the material Universe; and that it concludes with subtle fluids, each thinner than the other, in order to explain (i.e. make pictures of) the acts and properties of the miraculous Solids, which in their turn, however, react by a fresh diminuendo as the constituents and explainers of the all-explaining fluids? What are mankind the worse, that the sole orthodox systems of Physics and Metaphysics, out of the pale of which there is no salvation for reason or common sense—what matters it that this system, assuming—not matter— ... but BODY, the semper [jam] datum, euphoriae gratiâ creatum, the mysterious Melchisedek of the Atomistic faith 'without father, without mother, without descent (or pedigree), having neither beginning of days nor end', does by a strange contradiction confound the distinction while it at once affirms and destroys the Identity or co-inherence of form and substance, the first on the second ab extra, resolving all Quality into Accidents of Quantity, as if the

Properties were stuck, pins in one, needles in another, and brooches in a third? What is all this to the world at large?
(4:758-59)

Using rhetorical questions, ironic pleonasm, and apophastic irony, Coleridge charges, once again, that the fallacies of the hypothetical physics and the heresies of natural theology were at the root of modern revolution. These doctrines were reputedly responsible for commercial excesses, for social inequity, and for atheism, and they threatened Christian civilization.

An undocumented indictment of materialism and of its adverse cultural effects, this passage focuses on one of the two major cruces of hypothetical physics: the presupposition that existence was made up of corpuscles.[13] Coleridge states that modern "Physiology" (another confusion of disciplines?) or materialism "sets out with a pure fiction, an ultimate particle," extrapolating from this presupposition and thus compounding an original error. But what might sound, at first, like incoherent rambling is really an erudite litany of the theories and proponents of corpuscular thought in the sixteenth and seventeenth centuries. In this satire on "minima" doctrine, Coleridge refers to "the blank miracle" (revered by all atomists); to the "causeless... praeternatural Hardness or infrangibility... of corpuscles" (J. C. Scaliger [c.1484-1558], Gassendi [1592-1655], and Hariot [1560-1621]); to "insensate moats... elevated into Demiurgic atoms" (Giordano Bruno [1548?-1600] and Liebnitz [1646-1716]); to the "indivisible yet space-comprehending minims" (Galileo [1564-1642], Hariot, Beeckman [1588-1637], and Boyle [1627-1691]); and to the "subtle fluids... [that] explain (i.e. make pictures of) the acts & properties of the miraculous Solids" (Hobbes [1588-1679], Gassendi, and Newton [1642-1727]). Although unannotated, these references show how well-versed Coleridge was on the subject.

The first of four thematic passages treating the history of ideas and the interrelationship between philosophy and culture follows this indictment. Coleridge postulates that, "the history of all civilized nations in all ages," and "the recorded experience of Mankind," in general, indicate "that the Taste and Character, the whole tone of Manners and Feeling, and above all the Religious (at least the Theological) and the Political tendencies of the public mind, have ever borne such a close correspondence, so distinct and evident an Analogy to the predominant system of speculative Philosophy, whatever it may chance to be, as must remain inexplicable, unless we admit not only a reaction and interdependence on both sides, but a powerful, tho' often indirect influence of the latter on all the former" (4:759). This passage marks a subtle, though important, development in his thinking. In the 1808 and 1816 Scales, he tried to determine the interrelationship between philosophy and culture. In 1808, he suggested that many seventeenth-century thinkers saw the Mechanical Philosophy and the Glorious Revolution as "kindred" movements and "common causes." Yet no causation was implied: philosophy and politics were allied closely and were equally affected by unspecified agents. This analogical view became a causative one, at least tentatively so, in 1816, when he conjectured that, "all History seems to favor . . . that in every age the speculative Philosophy in general acceptance, the metaphysical opinions that happen to be predominant, will influence the *Theology* of that age" (*LS* 103); and "Not only the Theology; but even the Fine Arts" (Copy G, 103n.). I suggested that the 1816 Scale superseded that of 1808 by extending the analogy from Theology (a richly connotative word in his lexicon) to the Fine Arts, and by using Renaissance art to illustrate the influence of Neoplatonism. The subjunctive verbal phrase "seem to suggest" and the transitive verb "influence," I noted, point to his indecisiveness. But, by 1817, he brings the weight of recorded to history to bear as evidence that there has been "a close correspondence" between philosophy and culture, and an interdependence between the two: the "indirect influence" of philosophy on culture (4:759). Through polarization, he argues that philosophy and culture are interdependent, the former being the more active agent.

An interpolated illustration from the 1816 Appendix E follows directly. Coleridge's ostensible purpose here is to show how Renaissance Neoplatonism was reflected in the naturalistic works of the Great Masters. To do this, he describes art history, fourteenth to sixteenth century, as an oscillation between Neoplatonic naturalism and various forms of artifice. The oscillating curve moves from Gothic and Romanesque sculpture and painting, upward to the Renaissance Masters, and then downward to the artificial style of the Baroque period. First, he evokes the images of "reliefless surfaces" and of "wiry outlines" (4:759), suggesting Romanesque and Byzantine tableaux, such as "The Birth of the Virgin," a dogmatic mosaic in Constantinople (c. 1300-1320).[14] Another example of the kind of early Christian art Coleridge seems to be alluding to is the twelfth-century statue of "Isaiah" in the monastery Church of Souillac; here, in view of the prophet's ultralineal and elongated form, the sculptor seems to have been more interested in presenting a dematerialized entity than a real person.[15] Coleridge's point seems to be that earlymedieval art valued theological content over anatomical correctness.

Observing how this prevailing philosophy was embodied in Renaissance art, especially in the works of Giotto (1276-1337), Michelangelo (1475-1564), Raphael (1483-1520), Titian (1477-1576), and Correggio (1494-1534), Coleridge contrasts Gothic art to the Neoplatonic revival, exemplified by Dante (1265-1321) and Petrarch (1304-1374). Renaissance humanism, aesthetic idealism, and the recrudescence of Neoplatonism, he contends, were the most significant aspects of this epoch, and the Fine Arts mirrored the pervasive spirit of the age.

Similarly, the decline of Neoplatonism could be detected in art. The Italian Baroque was dominated by the Carracci family and by the Academic School, both of which Coleridge derides as "characterised by a nominal, motionless, idealess Dogmatism ... [the laying-on] of 'inveterate likenesses' ... under the common-sense and mechanic Philosophy" (4:759). Like the Romanesque, Byzantine, and Gothic Schools, the Academic School of the Carracci family dedicated its efforts to religious dogmatism. Noted for their grandiose theological schemes and imitation of Renaissance styles, Anibale Carracci (1560-1609) and his assistants— whose work is exemplified by the "Diana Visits Endymion" in the Farnese Chapel, Rome—tried to blend, in one scholar's words, "the power of Michelangelo, the suavity of Raphael, the color of Titian, and the sensuousness of Correggio," but came up instead with an "artificial and uninspired" aggregation.[16]

Coleridge's criticism is acute. Seeing in the works of the Carraccis an embodiment of corpuscular physics, hence a corruption of the Neoplatonic imagination, he reiterates his theory of a direct relationship between philosophy, art, and society. The bastardized style of Sir Joshua Reynolds (1732-1792) further illustrates his thesis: Reynolds' "semiplatonism" descended from earlier artificial styles, such as that of the Academic School, exhibiting craftsmanship, not imagination. Although these few examples "are but the ribs, abutments and sea-marks of a long line of correspondence in the arts of Taste to the opposite coast of speculative Philosophy," they point, incontrovertibly, to a more than coincidental relationship between philosophy and art.

A second thesis, reiterated from the 1808 and 1816 Scales, proceeds from this analogical survey of art history. Religion, Coleridge writes, "is at all times the center of Gravity in the machine ... with and through which Philosophy acts on the community in general, the influence is still more manifest"(4:759-60). The language is carefully chosen. The words "Gravity" and "machine" criticize materialistic and Newtonian thought, cosmologies supplanting God from space and time, and replacing Him with mechanically self-regulating systems. Through ironic pleonasm,

Coleridge inveighs against cosmologists, from Galileo to the French materialists, for trying to degrade God into a machine:

> What indeed but the wages of Death can be expected from a Doctrine which degrades the Deity into a blank Hypothesis, and that Hypothesis of a clockwork-maker—say rather, the Hypopoiesis or suffection, fairly open to Darwin's sarcasm—the 15th part of the atmosphere perishes we know not how—therefore, there is a Green Dragon at the north-pole—a Godless Nature and a Natureless abstract God, now an extra-mundane homo magus, from whom the world *had* its being, the Allah of Mahometan [sic.] Mono-idolism, and now the Sunday, or red-letter name of Gravitation, wherever the Pater-omnipotens AEther is not employ'd instead. One good thing, however, we owe to this AEther—it detects the hollowness of the usual excuse of the Doctors of the corpuscular system that their attraction & repulsion are but fictions in a Memoria Technica, meant to connect, not explain, the phaenomena of which they are the generic exponents. With the truly great Kepler's Centripetal and Centrifugal agencies this really the case—the terms simply generalize the facts—But the very terms substituted and chosen instead imply causative agency; and I will hazard an assertion, that there is not a single character in the works of any modern Theorist, a disciple of Locke, Hartley, & Condillac, that will not be found to contain positions utterly subversive of this pretence [sic.]. (4:760)

It appears that his anger is misdirected at mechanists such as the physico-theologians who saw in the mechanical philosophy a "scientific" version of the ontological proof. To them, God is a great Geometer (Galileo), a divine mechanic (Newton), or a disinterested watchmaker (Derham and Paley). Each metaphor bespeaks piety and awe before God's omnipotence, but each presumptuously reduces the majesty of God to a human model which is inherently closed and limited. Coleridge was appalled by this reductive practice; yet, ironically, his actual quarrel is with the rational cosmologists who subscribed to a random, particulate view.

In his criticism of the atheistic and reductive propensities of the new science, Coleridge does not resort to an anti-scientific rebuttal. Rather, from his accommodative position, he restates his premise that the natural sciences will somehow corroborate orthodox theology. To reinforce this contention, he explains how recent advances in Chemistry, demonstrating the falsity of hypothetical physics by virtue of "mutual penetration & intus-susception," actually validate the precepts of the Dynamic Philosophy, the organic view that independent elements could be dynamically synthesized into new elements. Here, Coleridge advocates the anti-hypothetical position, inaugurated by Bacon and Boyle, which had devaluated the mechanistic view of the universe. Coleridge's apparent advocacy of Newtonian empiricism over atomistic physics is ironic, for he failed to realize that the very cosmology he contravened, rather than being a by-product of atomic thought, was actually of rationalistic, and especially of Newtonian, origin. This confusion arose from his bad habit of consolidating disparate ideas together under imprecise titles.

Asserting that the most useful, least conjectural theorem of "the higher Geometry" was actually "the one healthy & prosperous graft from the Platonic tree!" (4:760), Coleridge opposes Democritian atomism, extolling Plato's theory of matter as an ingenious structural hypothesis.[17] Coleridge thought Plato's application of geometry to basic chemistry, and his understanding of the dynamic relationship between elements set the stage for greater advances in the field. Further evidence for this supposition are the "brilliant discoveries of modern chemistry, from Stahl to Davy"—that is, from the former's *Theoria medica vera* (1707) to the latter's induction into the Royal Society (1820)—which "were made during the *suspension* of the mechanic Philosophy relatively [sic.] to chemical Theory" (4:760-761). From 1660 on, reputable physical scientists, notably those of the R.S.L., had replaced the unfounded premises of the mechanical physics with methods yielding greater experimental certitude.

In the third critical focus of the Letter, concerning the Social Contract (4:761-62), Coleridge contends that the longevity of a civilization was directly related to the rectitude of its political philosophy. Once again incorrectly blaming natural-rights philosophy on atomism, he argues that atomism "permeates the whole mass of our principles" and that this current condition threatens to reduce England to the state of America, the Americans being "a Herd" of people "without a History." Despite the current sociopolitical unrest, England can still boast of an unbroken and glorious cultural history, a tradition surviving the "evanescence" of historical reconstruction (4:761). In this light, he more accurately criticizes "the Political Dogmata" of natural-rights thinking as "a *fac-simile* of [Mechanical] doctrines" (underscoring mine), saying that anticonstitutional and non-absolutist doctrines invested too much power in the common man. From this viewpoint, society could be conceived of as a flux of individuals, of human corpuscles, each determined to fulfill his own design and each only nominally committed to the common good. Without traditional institutions, he thought, society would disintegrate into factions, special interests, and nonconformities.

Coleridge attacks "the writings of Locke," that "'Perilous stuff' that still weighs on the heart of Europe" (4:761). But it is again unclear if he is impugning *The Two Treatises* or *Human Understanding*. Irrespective of whichever he reproves, we can be certain that he detested any social theory postulating "The independent atoms of the state of nature [as] cluster[ing] around a common centre" and as making "a convention," with that convention, in turn, making "a constitution of Government" (4:761).

Obviously reading political science analogically, Coleridge uses metascientific tropes to describe social disintegration. Developing the analogy between corpuscular atoms and social disintegration, he mocks the redundancy and arbitrariness of social contractualism: how "the makers and the made make a contract, which ensures to the former a right of breaking it wherever it shall seem good to them"; how this contract "assigns to the govern'd an indefeasible sovereignty over their Governors"; and how, once this "one-sided compact is dissolved," the ruled would fall "abroad into ... *independent atoms*" (underscoring mine), until "a new constitution is made by them" (4:761). He cites two antagonists, Locke and Major John Cartwright (1740-1824), but the direct reference is to Rousseau's General Will, expounded in *The Social Contract* (1762).

Rousseau theorized that a social contract would allow each citizen to put "his person and all his power in common under the supreme direction of the general will, and, in our corporate capacity, we receive each member as an indivisible part of the whole."[18] Justifiably concerned that this was an idealistic, potentially-dangerous theory, Coleridge raises the possibility of collective hysteria through which "the most numerous popular assemblies, nay even whole nations, may at times be hurried away by the same passions, and under the dominion of a common error" (*F* 1:193).

Inadvertently, Coleridge uses one speculative ideal to attack another when he says that the French Revolution taught him to distinguish between Rousseau's finite consensus and "the pure will which flows from universal Reason" (193). Moreover, he argues that "the falsehood or nothingness of the whole system becomes manifest" if we consider that the attributes of a contractual will apply neither to "one Human Being" nor to any one "Society or assemblage of Human Beings," nor least of all to the "mixed multitude that makes up the PEOPLE" (193). Instead, such an ideal applies "entirely and exclusively to REASON [which] dwells in every man *potentially*, but actually and in perfect purity is found in no man and in no body of men" (194). These dogmatic errors had inspired "the vain, ignorant, and intoxicated populous" of France "to wild excesses and wilder expectations" — namely the September Massacres (1792), the Reign of Terror (1793-1794), and the pursuit of an ahistorical order, eventually clearing the way for "military despotism, for the satanic Government of Horror under the Jacobins, and of Terror under the Corsican" (194). Under these conditions, he writes in the "Rescue" Letter, when "the minority happens to consist of a Ruffian at the head of an army of Ruffians" (4:762), tyranny is inevitable.

From revolutionary idealism and ahistorical social theory, Coleridge turns to Locke, their reputed progenitor, and focuses on the premise that mankind's primeval state was naturally moral and independent and that the State existed solely to benefit the people:

> It is high time, my Lord! that the subjects of Xtian Government should be taught that neither historically nor morally, neither in right nor in fact, have men made the state but that the state & that alone makes them men—a truth that can be opposed by those only who confound the state with the few individuals who have taken on themselves the troublesome and thankless duty of guarding it against any practical exhibitions of their new statecraft: that the name of country is a mere sound, if it be not true that the Flux of Individuals in any one moment of existence is there for the sake of the state, far more that the state for them—tho' both positions are true proportionably—that the jus divinum of the [supreme] magistracy is a tenet that has been discredited only by a gross perversion of its sense; lastly, that states and kingdoms *grow*, and are not to be *made*, and that in all political revolutions, whether for the weal or chastisement of the nation, the People are but the sprigs and boughs in a forest tossed against each other by an agency in which their own will has the least share. As long as the principles in our Gentry and Clergy are grounded in a false Philosophy, which retains but the name of *Logic*, and has succeeded in rendering Metaphysics a word of opprobrium, all the Sunday and National schools in the world will not preclude Schism in the lower & middle Classes. The predominant Philosophy is the key note ....
> (4:762)

No historical evidence, he argues, proves that the State is servant of the people; States and kingdoms evolve organically and cannot be fabricated from the ruins of political revolution. Resting neither with the singular nor with the collective will, the destiny of a nation depends on "an agency in which their own will has the least share." But does this contradict his Augustinian resolution of foreknowledge and free will? Ironically, Rousseau propounded a kind of secular equivalent to Augustine's solution: in both schemes, the individual will is subsumed under, though not obliterated by, the all-encompassing Will. The crucial difference is that, for Augustine, this is God's Will, whereas, for Rousseau, it is a personified, self-regulating principle. It is evident that, in his haste to refute Rousseauist idealism, Coleridge inadvertently states that the individual had no share in God's omniscience, which is to refute the idea of sacramental communion, and cooperation, with God. Despite this lapse, the most important aspect of this passage is the assertion that "the predominant Philosophy *is* the key note" (underscoring mine), the earlier indecisiveness disappearing before the conviction that philosophy shapes the milieu.

The 1817 Scale comprises four stages in the history of ideas, each of which is either criticized or extolled: 1) the legacy of atomism and of sensationalist psychology, c. 1648-1754 (i.e., from the English Civil War and the Restoration to Condillac's *Traité des sensations* [1754]); 2) the history of art—medieval, Renaissance, Baroque—illustrating the naturalistic and spiritual influence of Neoplatonism (c. eighth century A.D. to 1792 [i.e., to the death of Joshua Reynolds]); 3) the flowering of the new science and its reputedly adverse effect on metaphysics and theology (c. sixteenth to the eighteenth century), along with the history of chemistry, from atomic to Neoplatonic phases (i.e., from Plato to Davy); and 4) the history of Social Contract Theory and its collateral relation to atomic-sensationalist theory (Locke to the authorial present, c. 1680-1817).

For Coleridge, modern history contained a succession of dialectically-interrelated epochs, evolving towards a theodicean fulfillment. In the 1818-1819 Scale, he outlined both his history of philosophy and philosophy of history.

4. 1819

The most coherent exposition of Coleridge's periodical historiography is contained in a series of fourteen lectures, December 14, 1818 to March 29, 1819. In this 1819 Scale, he presents philosophy, "historically, as an essential part of the history of man, as if it were the striving of a single mind, under very different circumstances indeed, and at different periods of its growth and development; but so that every new direction should have its cause and explanation, while all by reference to a common object is reduced to harmony of impression and total result" (*PL* 67-8). Coleridge senses an immanent purpose to mankind's philosophical endeavors, directing and orchestrating even the most disparate ideas into an historical ensemble.

After devoting seven lectures to the period from Creation to classical antiquity, and then up to the consolidation of Western Christendom (sixth century), Coleridge allocates the remaining six chapters (the fourteenth is summary) to the philosophical characters of the most significant epochs. The following delineation indicates that he conceived of the history of philosophy syncretically: the eighth lecture, sixth to the twelfth century (to Western society; the feudal system and papal hierarchy; the Jews' contribution to medieval thought; the establishment of the Universities; and the rise of scholasticism); the ninth lecture, ninth to the fourteenth century (to the Schoolmen and scholasticism); the tenth lecture, fifteenth to early sixteenth century (to the revival of classical research and *belles lettres*; the Reformation; the works of Erasmus and Luther; the Italian Platonists; the speculative, theological, and political thought generally); the eleventh lecture, sixteenth century (to the progress of opinions from Edward VI [reigned, 1547-1553] to the Republican or Golden Age of English letters, with special reference to Bacon [1561-1626]); the twelfth lecture, seventeenth century (to the rise of Dogmatical Materialism and its effect on religion, morality, and common sense); the thirteenth lecture, eighteenth to early nineteenth century (to the rise of German philosophy; Leibnitz [1646-1716], Kant [1724-1804], Schelling [1775-1854], and their intellectual indebtedness to Locke). Reinforcing its structural and chronological unity is the important thesis, briefly stated in 1817, that philosophy shapes culture and civilization.

Throughout this extensive survey, Coleridge retains the idea that cataclysmic events punctuated specific epochs. In the eleventh lecture, he explains that, "There are three great instructive events in history the reflection on which perhaps more than on any other part of human history will repay us by the lessons of wisdom and caution which they imply: I mean the Reformation, the Civil War, and the French Revolution" (318). Like Ranke, Coleridge believed that mankind might profit from these lessons and, through them, comprehend the moral purpose and direction of human history in a providential context.

5. 1830

The fifth periodical Scale, entitled "Regrets and Apprehensions," can be found in chapter seven of *On the Constitution of the Church and State*. The title is appropriate, from Coleridge's viewpoint, mainly because of the resurgence of natural-rights thought and the reform clamor (Catholic Emancipation, Slave Emancipation, Irish Independence, and suffrage) which made the 1830s a decade of social crisis. During this period of reform, his historical vision remained stalwartly conservative and theologically orthodox.

The 1830 Scale lacks detail but is more than a mere reiteration, for Coleridge changes the phrase "Brief history" (1816) to "*Moral* history" (underscoring mine; *CS* 64), the adjective "moral" reflecting his commitment to theological history. Thus, from the Declarative Act and Revolution of 1688, he traces another ideological oscillation: a crest and a trough representing the rise and fall of idealistic philosophy (i.e., natural-rights thought) and the predominance of corpuscular philosophy, respectively. From this familiar beginning, recapitulating appendix E of the 1816 Scale, he describes how the concept of the "Idea" had devolved since the time of the Areopagus Club and the heyday of conservative statesmanship, that is, since the time of Burke's Commonwealth forefathers: Harrington, Nevil, and Milton. Coleridge also contributes to the evolutionary debate, rejecting outright the "Ouran Outang theology ['theory,' 1st edn.] of the origin of the human race, substituted for the Book of Genesis, ch. I.-X" (66).

The theme of decaying philosophy and the contrast between modern theory and conservative values recur throughout Coleridge's historical writing. But the conclusion of the 1830 Scale contains some practical insight. We recall that, in previous Scales, he had resorted more to polemics than to concrete proposals for the mitigation of contemporary social and political problems. When he exhorts the Established clergy to revive Anglican tradition, calling religion the State's "centre of gravity" (70), and when he attacks modern theory, he obviously presents himself as a conservative historian. On this foundation, he proposes a program, albeit idealized, to counter what he coined the "plebification" of science and philosophy in the Mechanics Institutes and Nonconformist schools. As a remedy, he calls for the establishment of "a permanent, nationalized, learned order, a national clerisy or church ... an essential element of a rightly constituted nation, without which it wants the best security alike for its permanence and its progression" (69).

Only through the inculcation of Anglican dogma and of conservative politics, which he thought inextricable, could England hope to maintain its historical integrity. Not surprisingly, the "final intention" of the clerisy would be to reconstruct the past: "to preserve the stores, to guard the treasures, of past civilization, and thus to bind the present with the past; to perfect and add to the same, and thus to connect the present with the future" (43-4). Unlike the Jacobin's insulated history, the formula for clerisical historiography, according to Coleridge, neither annihilated the past nor projected, irresponsibly, into the future; rather, Coleridge sought "the true historical feeling": the sense of the nation as an organic, providentially-elected entity (67).

Although the 1830 Scale needs the kind of definition found in the compendious 1817 and 1819 Scales, it nonetheless reflects the consistency of Coleridge's thought: special creation is an element indispensable to his ancient history; Church and State were besieged by adversarial ideas, assumed to derive from corpuscular physics and to undermine the integrity of existing institutions; England is the sociocultural focus of Divine Providence; and, as a recrudescence of seventeenth-century Anglican Divinity, the clerisy would undertake educational, civil, and theological reform, while articulating conservative history.

6. 1833

The sixth Scale in the sequence is a recorded conversation of April 5, 1833. Throughout his commentary on modern history an assured faith in God's immanence resounds, alternating with anxiety about social and political ferment. Thus his *Weltanschauung* is a protracted philosophical struggle, dramatized by recurrent battles, not between armies, but between ideas and their purveyors. In the British Empire, Coleridge discerned the makings of a new millennium, gradually realizable through the spiritual formation of the populous. This recorded conversation conveys the sense of history as an inexorable manifestation of Providence, punctuated by ideological and revolutionary paroxysms:

> It is curious to trace the operations of the moral law of polarity in the history of politics, religion, &c. When the maximum of one tendency has been attained there is no gradual decrease, but a direct transition to its minimum, till the opposite tendency has attained its maximum; and then you see another corresponding revulsion. With the Restoration came in all at once the mechanico-corpuscular philosophy, which, with the increase of manufactures, trade, and arts, made every thing in philosophy, religion, and poetry objective; till, at length, attachment to mere external worldliness and forms got to its maximum,—when out burst the French revolution; and with it every thing became immediately subjective, without any object at all. The Rights of Man, and the Sovereignty of the People, were subject and object both. We are now, I think, on the turning point again. This Reform [i.e., parliamentary] seems the *ne plus ultra* of that tendency of the public mind which substitutes its own undefined notions or passions for real objects and historical actualities. There is not one of the ministers—except the one or two revolutionists among them—who has ever given us a hint, throughout this long struggle, as to *what* he really does believe will be the product of the bill .... [T]hey have actualized for a moment a wish, a fear, a passion, but not an idea.
> (*TT* 149-50)

Composed during the rebellious climate of the 1832 Reform Bill, and surveying the period from c. 1660 to 1832, this entry neatly subdivides one hundred and seventy-two years into three contiguous epochs, each characterized by a prevailing philosophy and a revolutionary turning point. As he did in 1819, he cites the Restoration, the French Revolution, and the Great Reform Bill as revolutionary axes. At each convergence point, the "spirit of the age" inverts to its ideological opposite.

As he had done with the ancient and classical past, Coleridge embeds the polarization scheme in modern history and comes up with a convenient, though simplistic, model. The most glaring deficiency of this approach, typical of idealistic periodization generally, is that it forces uniquely-complex phenomena into conformity with a preconceived design. Another problem, encountered in previous Scales, is Coleridge's imprecision with respect to philosophical ideas and schools. One must take into account, as we take a closer look at this document, that a recorded conversation is inevitably prone to faulty transcription; so the reader, encountering ambiguities, has to sort out categories.

With Locke vaguely in mind as the bridge between empiricism and natural-rights doctrine, Coleridge reasserts that mechanico-corpuscular philosophy inspired democratic idealism and caused the French Revolution, at which time everything became Idealistic. At the juncture of the Reform Bill, Coleridge intimates a transition from the current political climate, which he associated with Jacobinism, to its ideological opposite. This raises a number of closely-related questions: did he anticipate a revolution in the 1830s, followed by a counterrevolution? If he did, what sort of philosophy did he see as replacing democratic idealism? Did he envision the resurgence of corpuscular thought and an empirically-minded technocracy indifferent to human rights? Or did he anticipate a conservative reaction and further repression? The 1833 Scale leaves us wondering about whether he anticipated this instantaneous transvaluation as a constructive or destructive event.

The ambiguity issues largely from the fact that the ideological transvaluation of "idealism," the Jacobin extremism Coleridge feared, could be construed as materialism, but this would be illogical since he had assailed materialism consistently. The problem is simply a matter of definition: here, "idealism" denotes, not the kind of Neoplatonism associated with the Cambridge Platonists, but rather that which is associated with Cartesian rationalists and even with idealists like Berkeley. This kind of idealism also situates the ground of knowledge, not in God, but rather in the mind of man.

Although Coleridge's periodization of modern history is undermined by ambiguity and unevenness, it remains conceptually unified. In view of what was being produced in Germany at the time, it is evident that his use of the polarity logic was not as anachronistic as one might assume. And despite its ideological motivation, his universal history is nonetheless meritorious for its eclecticism.

As we shall see in the next chapter, the temptation of the Orosian solution proved too strong for Coleridge. In *Church and State*, he created a modern version of the *translatio imperii*, the theory that the power of imperial Rome, God's City on earth, would be handed down to successive empires.[19] In so doing, he would betray his affinity, not to Augustine who had objected to such close ties between mundane power and divine authority, but to Orosius and his successors, especially to Bossuet, all of whom identified mundane empires as temporal embodiments of God's kingdom. Doubtless the most problematic dimension of theological history, the "New Rome" theory was prone to serious abuses. Cultural election could be easily proclaimed to justify national ambition. The line between imperial theology and national self-interest was not clearly demarcated, the latter too often subverting the Church's proselytizing mission.

CHAPTER NINE

The Ideas of Church and State

Conjecturing that a dialectically-interdependent Church and State was a condition for social change, Coleridge re-endowed his political philosophy with a chiliastic dimension that, he hoped, would reveal "the great drama of an ever unfolding Providence" (*CS* 32). Thus, in *Church and State*, he reprises the role of cultural spokesman and oracle. However, as the third and nationalistic phase of his theodicy, this vision of the Church and State would be justifiably challenged for its *aprioristic* assumptions, and especially for the divinization of the Anglo-Saxon State. His contemporaries began to question the historicity of such a claim. Henry Nelson Coleridge, for example, in his preface to the 1839 edition, calls *Church and State* an "idealized history," while R. W. Church judges his historical approach original but impractical.[1]

Following the precedents of Niebuhr (1776-1831) and Dr. Thomas Arnold (1775-1842) who also believed that Coleridge confused "ideas" and "history" (*CS* 57n.), twentieth-century critics have echoed this sentiment. Crane Brinton, for one, challenges the philosophical assumption that the Constitution was an "antecedent reality which has produced all the historical forms a given state has assumed"; therefore, *Church and State* suffers from the introduction of "an unsolved problem in epistemology."[2] To Alfred Cobban, these metaphysical claims are inherently contradictory: "Unable either to reconcile history and philosophy into a broader view of both, or to keep them clearly apart, he falls into the common error of the idealist school by simply confusing them."[3] G. A. Wells concludes that this idealism avoided historical truth, especially with respect to religion.[4] Even a sympathetic scholar such as Robert O. Preyer finds the idealized political theory oversimplified and historically unverifiable.[5] Coleridge's idealism, John Colmer observes, is self-delusive. In *Church and State*, Coleridge mistakenly thought that he was returning to first principles when in fact "he was drawing certain deductions from the working of contemporary British institutions in the light of their historical development."[6]

The charge of ahistoricity pervades the criticism. Michael Moran faults Coleridge for generalizing from the history of political institutions and for endowing them, unjustifiably, with an "aura of sanctity," and W. H.

Walsh describes his philosophical approach to history as imprudent and overly speculative.[7] In his illuminating study of German idealism, G. N. G. Orsini complains that, although Coleridge adapted Kant's "regulative" and "constitutive" distinctions, he contradicted Kant on this part of his doctrine in *Church and State* (I will argue this to have been an intentional modification) by incorrectly reifying political institutions.[8] Although elucidating a number of praiseworthy features—e.g., the influence of *Church and State* on Newman, on F. D. Maurice, and on the Oxford Movement—John Coulson also draws attention to Coleridge's confusion about "ideas," refuting the contention that they are "self-evident truths" or "*a priori* conceptual principles."[9] Anthony John Harding completely rejects the idealistic premise: "We cannot now conceive of societies as pre-existent to their conventions, but only as defined by, and indeed formed by, those conventions."[10] The primary weakness of *Church and State*, for Stephen Prickett, is precisely Coleridge's failure to see the "idea" as only a hypothetical principle deduced from the history of sociopolitical institutions.[11]

The consensus among the anti-idealists—with the exception, perhaps, of Wells—is that Coleridge was perplexed by the distinction between ideas and history. Actually, this alleged confusion was a consequence of his intellectual purpose, for he had intended to write a theological history grounding temporal phenomena in Divine Ideas. For a Christian historian such as Coleridge, the idealistic dimension was absolutely essential to history conceived of as "the great drama of an ever unfolding Providence" (*CS* 32). The anti-idealists also tend to obfuscate Coleridge's comprehensive intention to subsume the empirical under the idealistic perspective: he deliberately practiced a speculative, rather than quantitative, historiography, an approach imposing a preconceived and dogmatic framework on an already restricted field of historical data.

Though these critics illuminate a crucial deficiency in *aprioristic* history, none of them appropriately situates Coleridge's political history in a greater, theological context. Consequently, his historical thought has been disconnected from the Orosian-Bossuesque tradition and incorrectly evaluated in the context of German idealism, which is precisely the error John Stuart Mill had made.[12] Exacerbating the confusion are those critics who have not only misplaced Coleridge's work historically, but who have also used his conservative idealism and Christian orthodoxy as a fixed target for their own special interests.[13]

Obversely, there are those who have extolled Coleridge's idealistic perspective, but their commentaries, however incisive, generally lack critical focus and depth. Examples of this include R. J. White's approbation that Coleridge's idealism transforms history from a rational or mechanical system, a "glorified newsreel" into a stereoscopic panorama or "epic of ideas."[14] Less figurative but just as commendatory is Charles R. Sanders' uncritical restatement of Coleridge's idealistic approach: "History should not be read for the mere facts, but for the general principles underneath them," for he believed that the object of historical research was to find "the unity which bound all ages together," a philosophical approach revealing "the nature of man and the laws of the universe."[15] Kathleen Coburn unqualifiedly describes Coleridge's intellectual method—his interest in "the vitality and growth of ideas"—as having allowed him to interpret intellectual history organically, causatively, and universally (Intro., *PL* 42). Reaffirming that the Coleridgean Idea is naturally both practical and prophetic, Russell Kirk assumes that, since the "existing state of things in England is only an approximation of the ideal," a "wise reformer" might pursue social reform heuristically.[16] Because Coleridge's historical method was guided, presumably, by "the ideas of reason," William F. Kennedy approves of it, as does David Calleo who writes how difficult it would be "to make much sense out of constitutional history without the aid of something like Coleridge's Idea."[17] Of the favorable critics cited, none has adequately explored Coleridge's philosophical purpose, his intellectual context, or his generic experimentation.

Robert O. Preyer was the first to analyze the subject on a large scale. He reiterates the favorable view (White to Coburn) that Coleridge saw history as a unified and dynamic process and appreciates his idealism for having added a "new dimension to the writing of history," one that, though not entirely valid, reflected a sincere belief in the cultural and spiritual qualities of the State.[18] Owen Barfield revitalizes Preyer's thesis that Coleridge's idealistic approach endowed history with philosophical and organic unity.[19] Restricting their critical scope to the German and Victorian contexts, however, Preyer and Barfield did not relate Coleridge's conjectures to scholastic precursors.

Critics such as R. J. White, Robert O. Preyer, John Bowle, Graham Hough, and S. V. Pradhan have recognized, but have failed to develop sufficiently, the theological basis of Coleridge's historical thought.[20] White correctly rejects John Stuart Mill's contention that Coleridge's historiography was Germanic and affirms, instead, the Scriptural basis of his speculations; and Preyer stresses the fact that Coleridge rejected the principles of German idealism whenever they controverted Anglican theology. Bowle perceptively identifies the political theory as an amalgam of the "Anglican ideal of the Commonwealth" (after the Burkean model), of the "Kantian ideal of morality," and of the "Platonic cult of the 'Idea' of Church and State." This amalgam represents "an insular and more sanguine conservatism," reflecting the best traditions of "Anglican Churchmanship," exemplified by Hooker, Jeremy Taylor, and Cudworth. Though Bowle's idea of an "amalgam" conveys Coleridge's eclecticism, it, too, needs to be revised. As I will demonstrate, Coleridge's philosophical strategy in *Church and State* was to interrelate three philosophical ideas dialectically—Kant's theory of historical ideas, the ideal of an Anglican Commonwealth, and the Orosian-Bossuesque idea of imperial theology—and then to subsume this construct under the omniscience of Divine Providence.

Closer to the mark is Graham Hough's observation that Coleridge's political idealism was "more Platonic than Kantian and more Christian than either" (although I would substitute "Neoplatonic" for "Platonic"). The "regulative principle of all Coleridge's philosophical activity," he maintains, "was to make his idealist thought a secure base for Christianity"; hence, "the main function of the Church as a human institution is the advancement of knowledge, the instruction and civilizing of the nation." I wish to revise Hough's interpretation as well: Coleridge's idealism was Neoplatonic and, therefore, more Thomist than Kantian; and Kant's historical method would interest Coleridge only in terms of how it could be used to reinforce an imperial theology. The fifth critic in this group, S.V. Pradhan, recognizes that "Coleridge's philosophy of history is idealistic" and belongs to the "Christian tradition of historiography." He also alludes to Coleridge's eclecticism: how he modified the medieval perspective by placing greater emphasis on the interplay of human actions and historical events.

Those critics who have identified Christianity as the focus of Coleridge's historical thought direct us towards a comprehensive understanding of his strategy. Pursuing a unified yet pluralistic vision of political society informed by conservative nationalism and Trinitarianism, Coleridge's had a fourfold purpose: to preserve, rather than to sacralize, the authority of the State; to avoid absolute theocracy by using the regulative or Kantian idea, in part one of *Church and State*; to safeguard against Erastianism by sacralizing the idea of the Christian Church; and to affirm, through the "Tri-une" idea in part two, the ethical, inviolable, and supramundane character of the Christian Church. This calculated use of Ideas—of the Platonic-Kantian and of the Neoplatonic Christian—satisfies *both* his political *and* his theological imperatives and supports the interdependency of the Ideas of the National Church and the State, the sociocultural mission of the former and the civilizing obligation of the latter. This eclectic construct is, in turn, dialectically opposed to the chiliastic element in the equation—the Idea of the Christian Church—which is an extrinsic moral regulator, embodying and revealing God's salvific plan.

More theoretically than practically successful, the philosophical infrastructure of Coleridge's City of God belongs to the tradition of Orosius and Bossuet. Yet it is more than a mere recapitulation of outmoded forms, for the adaptation of Kantian epistemology to British history, and the assimilation of both into a Scriptural framework, evidence Coleridge's eclectic erudition. Although the strength of *Church and State* lies neither in scrupulous research nor in reasoned induction (*CS* 58), it remains an essential aspect of his theological history, nonetheless, and an important experiment in the history of ideas, the initial phase of which was Coleridge's adaptation of Kantian epistemology to his orthodox paradigm.

1. Kant's Theory of Ideas

Kant proposed that *a priori* knowledge, instead of being temporally anterior to experience as was commonly held in Neoplatonic circles, emerged from within the mind at the instant of sense impression and existed independently of the reason;[21] thus, in his *Critique of Pure Reason* (1st edn. 1781; 2nd edn. 1787), he located supratemporal Ideas "completely outside the limits of possible experience." Such "transcendental ideas," he reasons, "ought never to be employed as constitutive, such an employment being wholly sophistical" (A:640-3; B:668-71).

Believing that Ideas have a single, regulative function, and thus declaring the Reason to be a "deceptive extension" of the understanding that exceeded the limits of possible experience (A:295; B:352), Kant postulates that pure concepts of the understanding retain their validity only when referring to appearances or phenomena rather than to things-in-themselves or noumena, the apprehension of which exceeded experience. Any attempt, therefore, to attribute unity, substantiality, causality, or any other category to transcendental subjects—including the soul or God—would be spurious.

Even though Kantian Ideas could not furnish knowledge of reality in itself, they could still function "regulatively," providing the inquiring mind with rules, methods, laws, and direction. With respect to idealized goals, then, Ideas direct and support the understanding (A:640-3; B:668-71). But by far the most important distinction Kant made was that, although idealized goals could never be realized, they could still be approximated, the ultimate aim remaining "a purely imaginary point, a mere idea" (A:644; B:674).[22] He applied this rational epistemology to theology and history.

Kant believed that, despite human limitations, the historical presence of regulative Ideas could be inferred in the light of their ostensible purposes. Because they were definitively supramundane, however, historical Ideas could never be deduced from historical events (thus the Idea of "Cosmopolitanism" could only be understood imperfectly and indirectly).[23] Yet a philosophical historian, thought Kant, could still write history *according* to the Idea and, in so doing, guide mankind along the arduous path to its fullest realization.[24]

Kant explicates his theory of historical Ideas in Thesis Nine of his "Idea for a Universal History from a Cosmopolitan View" (1784). Here, he explains that, although one cannot apprehend historical processes phenomenally, a unifying Idea can be presupposed as existing, to "serve as a guiding thread for presenting as a system, at least in broad outlines, what would otherwise be a planless conglomeration of human actions" (24). Here, Kant is grappling with the idealist's dilemma of having to reconcile preconceived ideas with actual history. Not surprisingly, when he discusses the constitution of States, his rejection of *aprioristic* history contradicts his practice. A rationalized version of theological history emerges, having teleological and prospective features:

> if ... one carries through this study, a guiding thread will be revealed. It can serve not only for clarifying the confused play of things human, and not only for the art of prophesying later political changes (which could be reasonably hoped for without the presupposition of a natural plan) in which there will be exhibited in the distance how the human race finally achieves the condition in which all the seeds planted in it by Nature can fully develop and in which the destiny of the race can be fulfilled here on earth ... That I would want to displace the work of practicing empirical historians with this Idea of world history, which is to some extent based upon an a priori principle, would be a misinterpretation of my intention. It is only suggestion of what a philosophical mind (which would have to be well versed in history) could essay from another point of view ....
> (24-5)

Since Kant's "regulative" Idea—imposed upon, or deduced from, historical phenomena—has no firmly-demonstrable basis in reality, the question arises: if ideas or pure forms cannot be apprehended directly, and if their existence can only be inferred in the light of ostensible purposes, how then can an historical teleology—moral, natural, or supernatural—be logically deduced, or extrapolated, from phenomena? The question is rhetorical: such assumptions are fundamentally conjectural, a fact that Kant acknowledged.

Apparently, Kant's wariness did not dissuade Coleridge from finding in his "guiding thread" a potentially useful way of articulating the secular aspect of his historical equation; Coleridge adapted it, with foreseeable consequences, to his historiography in *Church and State*.

2. Coleridge's "Tri-une" Idea

Coleridge borrowed the adjectives "regulative" and "constitutive" directly from the *Critique of Pure Reason* (A:180;B:222), but he altered their epistemological values. Kant had said that the "regulative" Idea (a Platonic derivative) was purely transcendental and non-empirical. Though capable of prescribing moral conduct and of disclosing knowledge inductively, these modes could approximate, never embody, an ineluctable Idea.[25] On the other hand, for Kant, the "constitutive" Idea (an Aristotelian-Plotinian derivative) defined the nature of a thing, shared in its phenomenal being, was empirically perceptible, and had creative power. It is at this juncture that Coleridge diverged radically from Kant.

Coleridge's major innovation was to subsume the "regulative" *and* the "constitutive" values under a third aspect, the "intradeical" or Neoplatonic dimension of the Idea.[26] Christian Neoplatonists—such as Sts. Augustine, Thomas, and Bonaventure—argued that God created the world in accordance with His archetypal Ideas and that all Ideas necessarily subsist in, and emanate from, the Divine Mind.[27] St. Thomas, for example, said that Ideas exist independently in the mind of God (*ante rem*), in things as common characters (*in rebus*), and in our minds as concepts formed through the power of abstraction (*post rem*).[28] Unlike Kant's rational theology, Coleridge's moral theology, grounding all knowledge and existence in God, emphasizes mankind's spiritual communication with, and sacramental participation in, divinity. One dimension of God's revealed self is divine omniscience, an article of faith Coleridge professes to Thomas Clarkson: "God's Thoughts are all consummately adequate Ideas, which are all incomparably more *real* than what we call *Things*. God is the sole self-comprehending Being" (*CL* 2:1195-96)

Coleridge's assimilation of the regulative and constitutive values into the intradeical forms a unitary concept I call the "Tri-une" Idea. This ambitious merging of elements from the Platonic-Kantian, Aristotelian-

Plotinian, and Scholastic traditions, though articulated intermittently, is consistently expressed as an indivisible trichotomy.

Insofar as the "regulative" value was concerned, Coleridge agreed with Kant: a "regulative" Idea guides intellectual activity or moral behavior towards a pure Idea, one that could be mundanely approximated but never realized. Of the Idea's generative capability, Coleridge writes, "every principle is actualized by an Idea; and every idea is living, productive, partaketh of infinity, as (as Bacon has sublimely observed) containeth an endless power of semination" (*LS* 24). Moreover, Ideas are the wellspring of conscience: through the God-given faculty of Reason, man apprehends self-evident moral Ideas "without which the conscience itself would be baseless and contradictory" (*F* 1:112).

Regulative Ideas promote scientific experimentation, leading to the formulation of natural laws. Hence, the inclination "to universalize any phaenomenon involves the prior assumption of some efficient law in nature [correlative to the *apriori* idea], which in a thousand different forms is evermore one and the same; entire in each, yet comprehending all .... It is *attributed*, never derived .... Now a law and an idea are correlative terms, and differ only as object and subject, as being and truth" (*F* 1:467). Coleridge seems to be suggesting that the idea of a natural principle directs the investigator, empirically, to the formulation of natural laws; thus the scientific method is an inductive process that begins with a deductive premise, one that has been intuited and that can be approximated gradually. Through natural experimentation, he thought, the "*laws* of organic nature" are formed (1:470). Coleridge adduces an *a priori* "master IDEA," dimly apprehended through experimentation and warns that unless these Ideas are concretized—i.e., "if they do not lead to some LAW"—scientific discoveries "may remain for ages limited in their uses, insecure and unproductive" (1:478).

The "constitutive" value of the Idea, in Coleridge's view, is both descriptive and prescriptive; but the Idea-as-constituent supersedes the regulative value: "An IDEA, in the *highest* sense of that word, cannot be conveyed but by a *symbol*" (*BL* 1:156). An aesthetic correlative to the scientific law, the symbol reveals "the Universal in the Individual ... the Glance and Exponent of the indwelling Power" (*CN* 3:4397). Whereas the Hebrew legislators intuited "their particular rules as prescripts flow[ing] from principles and ideas that are ... reason itself" (*LS* 17)—that is, directly from the Absolute Will—modern philosophers contemplate the symbol, which is characterized "by the translucence of the Eternal through and in the Temporal"; moreover, it partakes of "the Reality which it renders intelligible ... enunciat[ing] the whole," and abiding "itself as a living part in that Unity, of which it is representative" (*LS* 30).

Coleridge's theological adaptation of Kantian epistemology is congruent with his description of imaginative creation, essentially the concretizing of Ideas or the process of making the regulative value constitutive. In Scripture, the imagination is a "reconciling and mediatory power," incorporating "the Reason in Images of the Sense," and organizing "the flux of the Senses by the permanence and self-circling energies of the Reason" (*LS* 29). Reason is itself an "organ of inward sense" and the power of acquaintance "with invisible realities or spiritual objects" (*F* 1:156). In turn, this process engenders "a system of symbols, harmonious in themselves, and consubstantial with the truths, of which they are the *conductors*" (*LS* 29). Coleridge sounds like he is describing the workings of the Secondary Imagination which "dissolves, diffuses, dissipates, in order to recreate; or where this process is rendered impossible, yet still ... struggles to idealize and unify" (*BL* 1:304). On a deeper level, the Primary Imagination, the medium through which Divine Ideas are intuited, establishes the intradeical ground of Ideas: it is "the living Power and prime Agent of all human Perception, and as a repetition in the finite mind of the eternal act of creation in the infinite I AM" (1:304).

J. Robert Barth elucidates the religious possibilities of the symbolic Idea. For Coleridge, the act of "perceiving" or of "making" symbols was an "act of faith ... necessary to perceive the true unity of being—the consubstantiality—with the differences"; and since an act of faith was a commitment through symbolic means, "the 'true' symbol for Coleridge might be said to be 'sacramental' "—that is, to be "a way in which God shares his power; it is finite participation in the infinite act of the I AM."[29]

3. Ideas in *Church and State*

Before studying Coleridge's use of the Kantian regulative Idea, we have to understand what he meant by the word "Church." In his lexicon, the "Church" has three meanings: the "National Church," an ecclesiastical endowment of the State and the focus of *Church and State*, part one; the ecumenical "Christian Church," the sum of all Churches and the focus of part two; and the "Church of Christ," a supratemporal category whose membership is known only to God.[30] Of these distinctions, that between the National and Christian Church is most essential to our understanding of Coleridge's purpose: to assert the providentially-ordained character of historical institutions in England.

The Idea of the National Church is an aspect, and subsidiary, of the State. In the Henrician tradition, Coleridge subscribes to Erastianism: the State "includes the National Church" (*CS* 73); yet he also maintains the concept of Church-State interdependence, which he acknowledges to be "a Truth of the highest practical importance" (*M* 1:360).

Since interdependency does not imply equality, these relationships do not appear to be contradictory. But the problem of interdependency was only a corollary to Coleridge's philosophical revaluation of historical categories. What really mattered was to preclude the reification of secular institutions but to do so *without* minimizing their teleological importance. He thought that a secular institution in England—even an ecclesiastical one like the National Church—was guided by an immanent purpose, known only to God, and dimly discerned by an enlightened few. Thus, with respect to the National Church and State, he had to find a way of describing the *civitas terrena* teleologically, *without* attributing to it the supernatural properties reserved for the "Christian Church" whose temporal manifestations he sacramentalizes. Like Augustine, he understood the danger of the divinized State, but like Orosius he, too, believed that God worked concretely through social history.

To explain how historical institutions developed within the divine ontology, Coleridge appropriated Kant's "regulative" Idea for use in part one *only*. Unfortunately, the half-dozen instances of its use contain a contradiction: Coleridge refuses to acknowledge the difficulty of attempting to deduce divine purpose from political history. In one example, on the grounds that reality can only approximate a reified "Idea," he differentiates the "Idea" of the Constitution from its historical manifestations. But then he asserts that "the constitution has real existence, and does not the less exist in reality, because it *is*, and *exists as*, an IDEA" (*CS* 19). The "Idea" of the Constitution, just like its historical manifestations "from Alfred onward," is real because it exists in the mind. The Idea and its historical manifestation, he seems to be saying, differ in kind only, but he does not clarify this crucial distinction. In another example, he claims to ruminate neither on "the history nor on the *actual form* of the British Legislature; but on the *Ultimate* Aims implied in the Constitution of the Same, by which [alone] as the regulative Idea, it can be rendered intelligible, and in reference to which as to its Criterion, it must be judged" (31n.). The question immediately to arise is: how does one learn about constitutional history in the first place? Certainly, one studies historical instances of it. But even if one studies the idea of constitutionality in the abstract, one must still refer to real concepts, articulated by real people, who lived in real times, and whose opinions were shaped by real conditions. The point is that, in this context, Coleridge appears to have made a false distinction between "Ideas" and their temporal manifestations, both of which are dynamically conditioned by events in time. Perhaps he is arguing for the genetic quality of ideas: if human ideas derive imperfectly from Divine Ideas, then human institutions, based on such inherited concepts, imperfectly mirror divine knowledge? But this can only be inferred.

The upshot is that Coleridge's appropriation of the Kantian regulative "Idea" was intended to differentiate the historical essence of secular institutions from that of the Christian Church (which, in fact, it does), as well as to place them within the purview of God. However, this exercise yields categorical and contrived distinctions: the transcendental property of the regulative "Idea" removes it from history, bringing it into too close an affinity to the Divine Idea, from which it derives and must be carefully distinguished.

Unlike the Idea of the State, the Idea of the Christian Church embodies the Tri-une Idea. Coleridge contradistinguishes it from mundane institutions: the Christian Church is not "a KINGDOM, REALM (*royaume*), or STATE, (*sensu latiori*) of the WORLD, that is, of the aggregate ... of the kingdoms, states, realms, or bodies politic ... into which civilized man is distributed" (114). In particular, it refines the ethical virtues of worldly institutions, concentrating and focusing the "beneficent and humanizing" aims, tendencies, "and proper objects of the state," and "radiating them back in a higher quality" (115). The spiritual presence of the Idea of the Christian Church also "completes and strengthens the edifice of the state, without interference or commixture, in the mere act of laying and securing its own foundations" (115). In addition to these constructive possibilities, it requires autonomy: simply "to be let alone" (115). A distinctly moral and active institution, the Idea of the Christian Church would guide the State (assuming its regulative function) in the civilizing and culturing process.

Public rather than "secret," communal rather than esoteric, the Idea of the Christian Church is also a constitutive presence. Complementing its "publicity" is its global character: it exists "in every kingdom and state of the world, in the form of public communities [and] as a real and ostensible power" (116).

Subsuming the regulative and constitutive properties under the intradeical, Coleridge completes the Tri-une formulation. Unlike the Idea of the State, that of the Christian Church, as a spiritual presence in the world, exists in the mind of God and is the instrument by and through which the Divine Will is disclosed. In order to explain its intradeical nature, he resorts to natural analogies. Because it lacks a "visible head or sovereign," because of "the non-existence ... of any local or personal centre of unity, of any source of universal power," the Idea of the Christian Church is compared to the Keplerian-Newtonian axiom that there is "a centre in every point of matter and an absolute circumference no where" (118). On the basis of this analogy, Coleridge concludes that, unlike the Idea of the State, that of the Christian Church operates according to "the True system of the heavens" (119), an incontrovertible sign of its supramundaneness. Extending this physical analogy (perhaps perilously close to physico-theology), he includes the aggregative unity of the Christian Church — "the unitive relation of the churches to each other, and of each to all" (119-20) — and asserts that its manifestations are "equally *actual* indeed, but likewise equally IDEAL, *i.e.* mystic and supersensual" (120). A diversified aggregate, the Christian Church embodies the Absolute Will of God in the world, completely, perfectly, and equally present, both in its differentiae and unity.

Further evidence of its divine nature and mission is its dispensation of "*spiritual* power" through the revelation of "moral Ideas" (123). The discernment of "moral Ideas" allows the faithful to commune with God and to share in His plenitude. Coleridge explains, appositively, that the discernment of "moral Ideas" is, at the same time, a means of participating in God's being: "moral *Ideas*" are "the Idea of the Eternal, the Good, the True, the Holy," and these Ideas emanate from, and subsist in, God, "the Absoluteness and Reality (or real ground) of all ... [moral Ideas], for God is the "Supreme Spirit in which all these substantially *are*, and are *ONE*" (123). Emphasizing the ontological unity of Ideas in God, Coleridge concludes that the Idea of the Christian Church is the means by which one might commune with God. By virtue of his salvific and historical mission, it is the embodiment of the Tri-une Idea.

When Coleridge theologically re-shapes English sociopolitical history, he is not practicing "history" as it is understood in the modern sense, for religious and cultural convictions clearly inform and direct his speculations; he is certainly not researching historical sources in order to create an authentic picture of the Church and State. His interest is primarily theological, for he is intent upon opposing the German idealists and others who had rationalized God into an abstract, nominally-benevolent force; thus he hoped to recover lost ontological ground through the recrudescence of scholastic doctrine, reinstating God as the Lord of history. Owing more to St. Augustine than to Fichte or Hegel, his theological history diverged, sharply, from empirical currents in historical research.

CHAPTER TEN

The Problem of Historical Knowledge

Coleridge's historical scope in *Church and State* contracts, progressively, from an already delimited global perspective to the parameters of the Anglo-Saxon imperium. His universal vision failing for want of ability, not of purpose, he could only reiterate the aphorisms that "Christianity" was a "providential" gift to the National Church (*CS* 55), and (citing Prov. 29:18) that vision is essential to a "Universal History" (58).

Coleridge's concern for human suffering, however, was authentic and impassioned. It seems that, once freed from paradigmatic abstraction, he could see the world from a human perspective, and what he saw disturbed him. Thus he sympathized with his impoverished countrymen who suffered from the effects of bad legislation and poor working conditions, enrooted inequities frustrating practical amelioration. As in 1798, a sense of perplexity and powerlessness pervades his voice. In the 1830s, the question he seems to ask himself is: what practical good can a philosophical tract serve during the years of the Reform crisis? Frustrated by his inability to affect the inhumane conditions of his times, he devaluates *Church and State* into "a catalogue *raissoné* of texts and theses," an outline for which, he hopes, others will supply the commentary (58). His discursive and imaginative powers ebbing, he could only lament the consequences of technological progress, documented in "a well-written history of the Inventions, Discoveries, Public Improvements, Docks, Railways, Canals" (*CS* 59). Industrialization, he believed—what he aptly called "the Dynasty of the Understanding" (59)—was exacting a terrible human toll. Civilization was degrading rather than reinforcing culture, thus creating conditions under which theological history seemed obsolete and replaceable by utilitarian treatises.

Coleridge remonstrates about the "*ultimate* ends" of this destructive process. "Where," he asks, shall we find "the historiographer of REASON," one, like St. Augustine who could reconstruct universal history before a fallen Rome? Convinced that crime statistics and Malthusian population theory were no substitutes for clerisical historiography (60), Coleridge reiterates his faith in the fortitude and resiliency of the human character and adverts to "a Protestant Church Establishment" (75) as the sole authority under which "the progressive amelioration of mankind" might be realized (75). To enunciate this progressive vision, he revitalized the traditional theological history and, by appropriating ideas, attempted to modernize this genre. To begin to understand Coleridge's historical perspective, then, one must trace his thinking back to its generic roots in early Christian writing and consider how he tried to accommodate modern scientific, philosophical, and political theory to traditional ideas and forms. Though the results are not always logical and complete, we should not conclude that his historiography was an anachronism and a failure. There remains an important affinity to consider: how his historical thought relates to his English contemporaries.

1. Romantic Historical Thought:
   The Problem of Teleological Relativism

The scholarly consensus is that Romantic historical thought was a reaction to Enlightenment historiography—to a tradition that emphasized rationalism, secularism, and universality but that failed to provide a viable formula for historical causality. R. G. Collingwood believes that the Romantics (both English and German) widened the scope of history through a more sympathetic understanding of past ages and rejected the eighteenth-century idea that human nature was uniform and unchanging.[1] Along with the desire to see positive and relative value in even the most distant civilizations, thought Collingwood, the Romantics sought to uncover an immanent historical mechanism giving human experience purpose and continuity. This teleological process was expressed, more commonly, as the progressive development of human reason or as the education of man.

The Romantics' pursuit of what I call "teleological relativism"—the view that historical epochs and cultures are unique yet part of an immanent process—created unforeseen problems, for the incorporation of diverse civilizations into a preconceived system, whether idealistic or theological, secular or ecclesiastical, tended to subvert the relativistic view. The Romantics' treatment of the Middle Ages provides a case in point. Alfred Cobban explains that Wordsworth, Southey, Coleridge, and Scott, in line with Burke, idealized the Middle Ages for the sense of "national community" they found in the feudal State.[2] For only from such a selective and idealized interpretation of the Middle Ages could they distill the coherent political principle of permanence and development. Pursuing a constructive solution to the problems created by eighteenth-century individualism and by economic imperatives—trends they viewed as deleterious to the Church and State—they recreated the history of the Middle Ages, artificially, in the light of their own experience, present needs, and wishes for the future.

Some scholars see teleological relativism positively. Acknowledging that the Romantics used an anti-historical approach, Butterfield accentuates their innovations, emphasizing the positive features of the Romantic reaction.[3] Noting the interpretative dangers of accepting such historiography uncritically, he points to the overriding explanatory and visual qualities of Romantic historical literature, attributing the Romantics' unusual blend of scientific rationalism and of fanciful preconception to a paucity of knowledge—to the fact that historical scholarship was then in its infancy. Butterfield rightly argues that Romantic theory was transitional and that more quantified research methods would develop from their work. Hayden White reaffirms the idea that the Romantics tried "to rethink the problem of historical knowledge" metaphorically, and the problem of historical process affectively—that is, in terms of "the individual conceived as the sole agent of causal efficacy in that process."[4] When working metaphorically and affectively, the Romantic writer approached historical data sympathetically and creatively, at the expense, however, of accuracy. Though White concedes that historical actualities were, at times, made to conform to preconceived political and ideological beliefs, sometimes confusing fact and myth, the Romantics' emphasis upon the role of the sympathetic imagination in the writing of history was very important. In fact, Romanticism's distinctive contribution to the field of historical philosophy, he points out, is precisely this regard for "individual human consciousness as a causal force in the historical process."[5]

With respect to the problem of historical knowledge at the beginning of the nineteenth century, the center of gravity had shifted too far away from the objective phenomenon to the subjective intelligence. In no place is this shift more clearly illustrated than in Romantic apocalypticism. M. H. Abrams has written prolifically on the subject, so we need only recapitulate that the French Revolution revived in the German and English Romantics the hope for a secular redemption.[6] For the English, the Revolution rekindled ideals inherited from the Puritan millenarianism during the Civil War; and, for the Germans, influenced by an older chiliastic tradition, there was a revival of interest in Pietist theology. But when the Revolution failed to fulfill prophecy, the Romantics disengaged themselves, imaginatively, from the unfolding political reality, a retreat illustrating Georg Iggers' notion of the fluid border between history, ideology, and myth.[7] After this recantation, Romantics like Blake, Wordsworth, and Coleridge internalized their visions of social eschatology, reformulating these processes into cognitive and revelatory terms.

Modern theorists who have analyzed the problem of historical knowledge can help us to understand why the Romantic emphasis upon idealistic and theological imperatives inevitably attenuated their historical capabilities. Modern theory demonstrates how complex historical speculation can be. Even for an historian claiming objectivity, there are epistemological variables that must be recognized and accounted for. Carl L. Becker, for example, distinguishes between the past event (ephemeral and irrecoverable), an affirmation of this event (historical documents or oral tradition, ontologically removed from it), and the historical interpreter himself (conditioned by the milieu).[8] Yet, under these epistemological circumstances, Becker concludes, the historical explanation depends largely on the interpreter: "It is the historian who speaks, who imposes a meaning." Becker's dialectical outline and the lively debate over relativistic historiography suggest the intrinsically problematic nature of the teleological approach.

Coleridge's theological history, then, is properly understood as a product of his age and, as such, reflects the paradox of Romantic historiography: the illusion of teleological relativism. Coleridge reasserts constructive social values and the tradition of Church and State interdependency, but he does so uncritically, abstractly, and monolithically, subordinating cultural relativism to a theological paradigm. The strength of his approach to history is its wide-ranging eclecticism and the conviction that human knowledge and experience can be synthesized to reveal a deeper purpose. Although Coleridge's intellectual constructs and formulae are, at times, fragmentary and sketchy, his historical thought—with its interdisciplinary and synthetic character—remains a valuable and unrecognized contribution to the development of historiography.

NOTES

NOTES TO CHAPTER ONE

1. Max F. Schulz, "Samuel Taylor Coleridge," in *The English Romantic Poets: A Review of Research and Criticism*, ed. Frank Jordan, 4th edn. (New York: The Modern Language Association of America, 1985), 427.
2. "The Theology of History," *New Catholic Encyclopedia*, 17 vols. (New York: McGraw Hill, 1967), 7:26. For descriptions of the genre and of its origins, I am entirely indebted to R. G. Collingwood, *The Idea of History* (1946; rpt. New York: Oxford UP, 1974), 46-56; to M. H. Abrams, *Natural Supernaturalism: Tradition and Revolution in Romantic Literature* (New York: Norton, 1971), 32-37; to Herbert Butterfield, *The Origins of History*, ed. Adam Watson (New York: Basic Books, 1981), 158-64; to Ernst Breisach, *Historiography: Ancient, Medieval and Modern* (Chicago and London: The Univ. of Chicago Press, 1983), 77-88; to M. C. D'Arcy, S.J., *The Meaning and Matter of History: A Christian View* (1959; rpt. New York: The Noonday Press, 1967), 79-121; to Robert Paul Mohan, *Philosophy of History: An Introduction. Horizons in Philosophy*, gen. eds. Jude Dougherty and Robert Wood (New York: Bruce Pub. Co., 1970), 143-61; and to Hug, 7:26-30.
3. Norman Cohn. *The Pursuit of the Millennium* (New York: Oxford Up, 1977), 15; Ernest Tuveson, "Millenarianism," *DHI*, 3:222a-225b; and Peter Kitson, "Coleridge, Milton, and the Millennium," *The Wordsworth Circle*, 18.2 (Spring 1987): 63-5.
4. Abrams, 329-34.
5. Richard Haven, *Patterns of Consciousness: An Essay on Coleridge* (Amherst, MA: Univ. of Massachusetts Press, 1969), 7-8; Laurence S. Lockridge, "Explaining Coleridge's Explanation: Toward A Practical Methodology for Coleridge Studies," in *Reading Coleridge: Approaches and Applications*, ed. Walter B. Crawford (Ithaca and London: Cornell UP, 1979), 34, 47.

NOTES TO CHAPTER TWO

1. Jean Daniélou, S.J., *The Lord of History: Reflections on the Inner Meaning of History*, trans. Nigel Abercrombie (London and Chicago: Longmans, Green and Henry Regnery, 1964), 24-6; Jürgen Moltmann, "Theology as Eschatology," in *The Future of Hope: Theology as Eschatology*, by Jürgen Moltmann et al., ed. Frederick Herzog (New York: Herder and Herder, 1970), 2.
2. For this background, I am indebted to Breisach, 77-88, and to Butterfield, *Origins*, 158-64.
3. Eusebius, *The History of the Church*, trans. and intro. G. A. Williamson (New York: Penguin, 1988), 22.

4 St. Augustine, *Concerning the City of God Against the Pagans*, trans. Henry Bettenson, intro. John O'Meara (New York: Penguin, 1984), 593-7.

5 Paulus Orosius, *Seven Books of History Against the Pagans*, trans. and intro. Irving Woodworth Raymond, no. 26 in *Records of Civilization: Sources and Studies*, gen. ed. Austin P. Evans, assoc. eds. Frederick Barry and John Dickinson (New York: Columbia UP, 1936).

6 Breisach, 86; and Peter Gay and Gerald J. Cavanaugh, eds. *Historians at Work*, 4 vols. (New York and London: Harper & Row, 1972), 1:315-17.

7 Breisach, 199.

8 For background, I am indebted to Michael Allen Gillespie, *Hegel, Heidegger, and the Ground of History* (Chicago and London: Univ. of Chicago Press, 1984), 9-17.

9 D'Arcy, 93-7.

10 Francois Marie Arouet de Voltaire, *The Portable Voltaire*, ed. Ben Ray Redman (New York: Penguin, 1984), 549.

11 Abrams, 201-17; Butterfield, *Man On His Past: The Study of the History of Historical Scholarship* (Boston: Beacon Press, 1966), 14-17, 34-9, 50-3, 56-61, 64-5, 72, 77, 88-9.

12 F. W. J. Schelling, *Philosophical Inquiries into the Nature of Human Freedom*, trans. and ed. James Gutmann (La Salle, Illinois: Open Court, 1936), 109-110.

13 Butterfield, *Man On His Past*, pp. 40-50.

14 Georg G. Iggers, *New Directions in European Historiography* (Middletown, CT: Wesleyan UP, 1984), 10.

15 Leopold von Ranke, "Preface" to *Histories of the Latin and Germanic Nations*, "A Fragment from the 1830s," and "A Fragment from the 1860s," in *The Varieties of History from Voltaire to the Present*, ed. and intro. Fritz Stern (New York: Vintage, 1973), 57, 59, 62.

NOTES TO CHAPTER THREE

1 Abrams, 265-7.

2 Leo Gershoy, *From Despotism to Revolution, 1763-1789*, vol. 10 of *The Rise of Modern Europe*, Ed. William L. Langer 20 vols. (New York: Harper & Row, 1944), 120-33, 174-81.

3 Carl R. Woodring, *Politics in the Poetry of Coleridge* (Madison: The Univ. of Wisconsin Press, 1961), 181.

4 Abrams, 364-7.

NOTES TO CHAPTER FOUR

1 Peter Gay, *The Science of Freedom*, Vol. 2 of *The Enlightenment: An Interpretation*, 2 vols. (New York: Norton, 1969), 319-20, 388-96.

2 In *Gibbon's Antagonism to Christianity* (London: Williams & Norgate, 1933), Shelby T. McCloy collects the major reactions to *The Decline and Fall and Fall of The Roman*

Empire (ed. Oliphant Smeaton, 3 vols. [New York: Modern Library, 1911], hereafter *D&F*), especially those emanating from Oxford and Cambridge, and tersely describes this ongoing debate as "The Gibbon Controversy." Centering on Gibbon's famous fifteenth and sixteenth chapters, the bulk of this material deals with his philosophical and theological arguments. McCloy's appraisal of Coleridge's reaction, long considered comprehensive, was echoed by G. M. Young (*Gibbon* [New York: Appleton, 1933], 132), and subsequently challenged by Kathleen Coburn who understates the case when she says that McCloy's view "needs modification" (*PL* 421n.).

The problem with McCloy's view is that it misleadingly emphasizes Coleridge's strident tone over more salient considerations (the phrase "savage criticism" is used [209]). Conveying the idea that Coleridge thoughtlessly relegated *The Decline and Fall* to "the realm of fable and anecdote" (249-50), McCloy dismisses his work as sweeping, caustic, and devoid of critical intelligence. Yet McCloy restricted his research on the subject to Coleridge's well-known *Table Talk* passage which is but a fragment of the corpus. His anti-Coleridgean bias is evident in his treatment of the critic, J. M. Robertson (1907), who had attacked the very same passage for its stridency, but who nonetheless conceded that some of Coleridge's observations— e.g., Gibbon's philosophical shallowness—were insightful after all (McCloy cites Robertson, 251). Angered by this concession, McCloy then attacked Robertson.

3 Northrup Frye, *The Great Code: The Bible and Literature* (New York: Harcourt Brace, 1981), 32.

4 Gay, *The Rise of Modern Paganism*, Vol. 1 of *The Enlightenment*, 385.

5 McCloy, 13-15, 60, 80, 90, 110-111, 118, 203, 230.

6 McCloy, 127, 249-51; Young, 132.

7 Gibbon criticized himself with respect to the style and ordonnance of *The Decline and Fall* and his pursuit of "the middle tone" (Edward Gibbon, *Autobiography*, ed. M. M. Reese [London: Routledge and Kegan Paul, 1970], 97-8).

8 Ernest Campbell Mossner, "Edward Gibbon," *The Encyclopedia of Philosophy*, ed. Paul Edwards, 8 vols. (New York and London: Macmillan & The Free Press, 1972), 3-4:328-29.

9 David Hume, *An Enquiry Concerning Human Understanding* (La Salle: Open Court, 1963), 97.

10 McCloy, 87.

11 Paul MacKendrick, H. H. Hexter, et al., *Western Civilization*, 2 vols. (New York: Harper & Row, 1968), 1:314-17.

12 Peter Gay, *Style in History* (New York: Basic Books, 1974), 54.

NOTES TO CHAPTER FIVE

1 J. Robert Barth, S.J., *Coleridge and Christian Doctrine* (Cambridge, MA: Harvard UP, 1969), 72-9.

2 *Samuel Taylor Coleridge: An Anthology*, ed. H. J. Jackson, Oxford Standard Authors, gen. ed. Frank Kermode (New York: Oxford UP, 1985), 565.

3 Barth, *Christian Doctrine*, 72.

4 Joseph A. Mazzeo, "Medieval Hermeneutics: Dante's Poetic of Historicity," *Religion and Literature*, 17.1 (Spring 1985): 10-11.

5 Anicius Manlius Serverinus Boethius, *The Consolation of Philosophy*, trans. Richard Green, The Library of the Liberal Arts (Indianapolis and New York: Bobbs-Merrill, 1962), 115.

6 J. Robert Barth, S.J., *The Symbolic Imagination: Coleridge and the Romantic Imagination*, Princeton Essays in Literature (Princeton: Princeton UP, 1977), 12-14.

7 Herbert Butterfield, *The Origins of Modern Science, 1300-1800* (New York: The Free Press, 1965), 232-33, 238; hereafter noted as *Science*; see also Marilyn Gaull, "Under Romantic Skies: Astronomy and the Poets," *The Wordsworth Circle*, 21:1 (Winter 1990): 34-5.

NOTES TO CHAPTER SIX

1 Robert M. Kingdon, "Determinism in Theology: Predestination," *DHI* 2:25-31.

2 Barth, *Christian Doctrine*, 123.

3 Augustine, 195.

4 Boethius, 130.

5 Barth, *Christian Doctrine*, 122-3.

NOTES TO CHAPTER SEVEN

1 Butterfield, *Man On His Past*, 16, 40-1.

2 Breisach, 185; Loren Eisley, *Darwin's Century: Evolution and the Men Who Discovered It* (Garden City, NY: Doubleday, 1961), 61; and Claude C. Albritton, Jr., *The Abyss of Time: Changing Conceptions of the Earth's Antiquity after the Sixteenth Century* (New York and Los Angeles: Jeremy P. Tarcher, 1986), 17, 57-77.

3 Basil Willey, *The Eighteenth-Century Background: Studies on the Idea of Nature in the Thought of the Period* (London: Chatto and Windus, 1957), 27-42; Thomas Hankins, *Science and the Enlightenment*, Cambridge History of Science Series, eds. George Basalla and William Coleman, 7 vols. (New York and London: Cambridge, UP), 4:115-17.

4 Eisley, 57-89, 91-115; Gaull, *English Romanticism: The Human Context* (New York and London: Norton, 1988), 351-76; and "Astronomy and the Poets," 34-5.

5 Trevor H. Levere, *Poetry Realized in Nature: Coleridge and Early Nineteenth-Century Science* (New York: Cambridge UP, 1981), 161-69.

6 Levere, 131.

7 Johann Friedrich Blumenbach, *Über die natürlichen Verschiedenheiten im Menschengeschlechte* . . . [Selections], in *Readings in Early Anthropology*, ed. J. S. Slotkin, Viking Fund Publications in Anthropology, 40 (Chicago: Aldine, 1965), 190. For

Coleridge's commentary on Blumenbach, see: *BL* 1:207n.; *CL* 1:472, 494, 497; *IS* 245; *CN* 2: 2544, 3:4047, 4273; and *M* 1:535-41.

8. *The Complete Works of Samuel Taylor Coleridge*, ed. W. G. T. Shedd, 7 vols. (New York: Harper and Brothers, 1884), 6:279.

9. J. H. Haeger, "Coleridge's Speculations on Race," *Studies in Romanticism*, 3 (1974): 356-7.

10. Stephen Jay Gould, *The Mismeasure of Man* (New York and London: Norton, 1981), 36-38.

11. Levere, 114-15.

12. Butterfield, *Man On His Past*, 55-6.

13. Barth, *Christian Doctrine*, 169-70.

14. Levere, 131.

15. Levere, 131-7.

16. Samuel Taylor Coleridge, "Note on 'Evolution'," in *Samuel Taylor Coleridge: The Selected Poetry and Prose*, ed. Stephen Potter (London: Nonesuch, 1962), 470.

17. See Craig Miller, "Coleridge's Concept of Nature," *The Journal of the History of Ideas*, 25 (1964):85; and John H. Muirhead, *Coleridge as Philosopher* (London: George Allen and Unwin, 1930), 130-6.

18. Kathleen Coburn, *The Self-Conscious Imagination* (London: Oxford UP, 1974), 64-5.

NOTES TO CHAPTER EIGHT

1. Johann Gottlieb Fichte, *Characteristics of the Present Age [17 lectures]; and the Way Towards the Blessed Life or the Doctrine of Religion*, vol. 2 of *The Popular Works of J. G. Fichte*, trans. William Smith, 4th edn. (London: Trübner, 1889); rpt. in *Significant Contributions to the History of Psychology, 1750-1920*, ed. David N. Robinson (Washington, D.C.: Univ. Publications of America, 1977); and Georg Wilhelm Friedrich Hegel, *The Philosophy of History*, intro. C. J. Friedrich, trans. J. Sibree (1837; rpt. New York: Dover, 1956).

2. Dietrich Gerhard, "Periodization in History," *DHI*, 3:476-81.

3. Peter Thorslev, *Romantic Contraries: Freedom versus Destiny* (New Haven and London: Yale UP, 1984), 36-7.

4. Robert H. Kargon, "Atomism in the Seventeenth Century," *DHI*, 1:132-41. See also Frederick Copleston, S.J., 9 vols., *A History of Philosophy* (Garden City, NY: Doubleday, 1963), 4:300-23; and Kargon, *Atomism in England: from Hariot to Newton* (Oxford: At the Clarendon Press, 1966).

5. John Locke, *An Essay Concerning Human Understanding*, ed. A. A. Woozley (New York: Meridian, 1964); and *The Two Treatises of Government*, ed. and intro. Peter Laslett (Cambridge: Cambridge UP, 1960).

6. Butterfield, *Science*, 194.

7. Laslett, intro., 58-80; Kargon, *DHI*, 1:140.

8. Michael Levin, "Social Contract," *DHI*, 4:251-63.
9. Laslett, intro., 45; and Jerzy Szacki, *A History of Sociological Thought*, Contributions in Sociology, 35 (Westport, CT: Greenwood Press, 1979), 45.
10. Norman Torrey, intro., *Les Philosophes: The Philosophers of the Enlightenment and Modern Democracy* [A Selection], ed. and intro. Norman L. Torrey (New York: Capricorn, 1960), 12.
11. Frederick B. Artz, *The Enlightenment in France* (Oberlin, OH: Kent State UP, 1968), 14.
12. William Flint Thrall, Addison Hubbard, and C. Hugh Holman, *A Handbook to Literature* (New York: Odyssey Press, 1960), 30.
13. Kargon, *DHI*, 1:138.
14. Bernard S. Myers, *Art and Civilization* (New York: McGraw-Hill, 1967), 166.
15. Myers, 166.
16. Myers, 270-1.
17. Harold J. Johnson, "Changing Concepts of Matter," *DHI*, 3:188.
18. Jean-Jacques Rousseau, *The Social Contract*, ed. and trans. Willmoore Kendall, 3rd edn. (Chicago: Henry Regnery, 1954), 15.
19. Breisach, 143.

NOTES TO CHAPTER NINE

1. Henry Nelson Coleridge, the 1839 Preface, *CS*, App. A, 196-7; R. W. Church, *The Oxford Movement: Twelve Years, 1833-1845*, ed. and intro. Geoffrey Best, Classics of British Historical Literature, gen. ed. John Clive (1891; rpt. Chicago and London: The Univ. of Chicago Press, 1970), 23-9.
2. Crane Brinton, *The Political Ideas of the English Romantics* (1926; New York: Russell and Russell, 1962), 76, 82.
3. Alfred Cobban, *Edmund Burke and the Revolt Against the Eighteenth Century* (London: George Allen and Unwin, 1929), 179.
4. G. A. Wells, "Herder's and Coleridge's Evaluation of the Historical Approach," *Modern Language Review*, 48 (April 1953):175.
5. Robert O. Preyer, "Coleridge's Historical Thought," *Coleridge: A Collection of Critical Essays*, ed. Kathleen Coburn (Englewood Cliffs, NJ: Prentice-Hall, 1967), 156, 159.
6. John Colmer, *Coleridge: Critic of Society* (Oxford: The Clarendon Press, 1959), 156; and *CS*, 57n.
7. Michael Moran, "Samuel Taylor Coleridge," *The Encyclopedia of Philosophy*, 2:137; W. H. Walsh, *Philosophy of History: An Introduction* (New York: Harper, 1967), 124n.
8. G. N. G. Orsini, *Coleridge and German Idealism* (Carbondale and Edwardsville: Southern Illinois UP, 1969), 131.
9. John Coulson, *Newman and the Common Tradition* (Oxford: The Clarendon Press, 1970), 23, 39.

10. Anthony John Harding, *Coleridge and the Idea of Love* (Cambridge: Cambridge UP, 1974), 206.
11. Stephen Prickett, *Romanticism and Religion* (London: Cambridge UP, 1979), 270.
12. John Stuart Mill, *On Bentham and Coleridge*, intro. F. R. Leavis (New York: Harper & Row, 1962), 108-09.
13. R. F. Storch, "The Politics of the Imagination," *Studies in Romanticism* (Fall 1982): 449-50, 455; Jerome McGann, *The Romantic Ideology: A Critical Investigation* (Chicago: Univ. of Chicago Press, 1983), 5-8; see also Anne K. Mellor "A Review of Jerome McGann's *The Romantic Ideology*," *Studies in Romanticism*, 25.2 (Summer 1986):284; and Michael Fischer, "Morality and History in Coleridge's Political Theory," *Studies in Romanticism*, 21 (Fall 1982):458, 460.
14. R. J. White, intro., *The Political Thought of Samuel Taylor Coleridge: A Selection*, ed. R. J. White (1938; London: Jonathan Cape, 1970), 21-2.
15. Charles R. Sanders, *Coleridge and the Broad Church Movement* (Durham: Duke UP, 1942), 54-5.
16. Russell Kirk, *The Conservative Mind: From Burke to Santayana* (London: Faber and Faber, 1954), 162, 164.
17. William F. Kennedy, *Humanist versus Economist: The Economic Thought of Samuel Taylor Coleridge*, Univ. of Calif. Publications in Economics, 17 (Berkeley and Los Angeles: Univ. of Calif. Press, 1958), 12; David Calleo, *Coleridge and the Idea of the Modern State*, Yale Studies in Political Science, 18 (New Haven: Yale UP, 1966), 89.
18. Robert O. Preyer, *Bentham, Coleridge, and the Science of History* (West Germany: Verlag Heinrich Pöppinghaus, 1958), 18-26, 77-82.
19. Owen Barfield, *What Coleridge Thought* (Middletown, CT: Wesleyan UP, 1971), 158-78, esp. 165; see also Raimonda Modiana, "Metaphysical Debate in Coleridge's Political Theory," *Studies in Romanticism*, 21 (Fall 1982):466, 469; Daniel M. McVeigh, "Political Vision in Coleridge's *The Statesman's Manual*," *The Wordsworth Circle*, 14.2 (Spring 1983):88, and "Coleridge's Doctrine of the Imagination and the Enigmatic Name of God," *Religion in Literature*, 17.1 (Spring 1985):66; Abrams, 329-34; Stuart Peterfreund, "Coleridge and the Politics of Critical Vision," *Studies in English Literature: 1500-1900*, 21.4 (Autumn 1981):588, 593-604; David Pym, *The Religious Thought of Samuel Taylor Coleridge*, foreword by John Coulson (New York: Barnes and Noble, 1979), 64-5; and Anthony John Harding, *Coleridge and the Inspired Word* (Kingston, Ontario: McGill-Queen's UP, 1985), 5-6, 20-1, 78.
20. John Bowle, *Politics and Opinion in the Nineteenth Century* (New York: Oxford UP, 1964), 91, 194; R. J. White, intro., *The Political Tracts of Wordsworth, Coleridge and Shelley* [Selections] (Cambridge: Cambridge UP, 1953), xii-xvi; Preyer, *Science of History*, 2-3; Graham Hough, "Coleridge and the Victorians," *The English Mind: Studies in the English Moralists Presented to Basil Willey*, eds. Hugh Sykes Davis and George Watson (Cambridge: Cambridge UP, 1964), 179-80; S. V. Pradhan, "The Historiographer of Reason: Coleridge's Philosophy of History," *Studies in Romanticism*, 25.1 (Spring 1986):57-9.
21. Copleston, 6.2:13; Orsini, 76-7; Immanuel Kant, *Critique of Pure Reason*, trans. F. Max Müller (1781; Garden City, NY: Anchor-Doubleday, 1966), 668-71.
22. Orsini, 130-1.

[23] Lewis White Beck, intro., *Kant on History*, by Immanuel Kant, ed. and trans. Lewis White Beck, et al., The Library of the Liberal Arts (Indianapolis and New York: Bobbs-Merrill, 1980), xviii-xx; Kant, "Idea for a Universal History from a Cosmopolitan Point of View," 24-5.

[24] Beck, xx-xxi.

[25] George Boas, "The Idea," *DHI*, 2:542-9.

[26] H. A. Wolfson's neologism: "within God"; cited by Orsini, 131.

[27] Etienne Gilson, *The Spirit of Medieval Philosophy*, The Gifford Lectures, 1931-1932, trans. A. H. C. Downs (1936; New York: Charles Scribner's Sons, 1940), 158-9.

[28] Boas, 546.

[29] Barth, *Symbolic Imagination*, 12-14.

[30] Cobban, 241; Barth, *Christian Doctrine*, 162-8.

NOTES TO CHAPTER TEN

[1] Collingwood, 86-8.

[2] Cobban, "The Revolt Against the Eighteenth Century," in *Romanticism and Consciousness*, 137-43.

[3] Butterfield, *Origins*, 35.

[4] Hayden V. White, *Metahistory: The Historical Imagination in Nineteenth-Century Europe* (Baltimore and London: The Johns Hopkins Press, 1973), 80.

[5] Hayden V. White, "Romanticism, Historicism, and Realism: Toward a Period Concept for Early 19th Century Intellectual History," in *The Uses of History: Essays in Intellectual and Social History*, presented to William J, Bossenbrook, compiled and ed. Alfred H. Kelly (Detroit: Wayne State UP, 1968), 50-1.

[6] Abrams, "Apocalypse: Theme and Romantic Variations," in *The Revelation of St. John the Divine: Modern Critical Interpretations*, ed. Harold Bloom (New York: Chelsea House, 1988), 25-6.

[7] Iggers, 4.

[8] Carl L. Becker, "What are Historical Facts?" in *The Philosophy of History in Our Time: An Anthology*, selected and ed. Hans Meyerhoff (Garden City, NY: Doubleday-Anchor, 1959), 131.